Portland Community Co

WITHDRAWN

ISSUES THAT CONCERN YOU

Performance-Enhancing Drugs

Tamara L. Roleff, *Book Editor*

GREENHAVEN PRESS
A part of Gale, Cengage Learning

GALE
CENGAGE Learning

Detroit • New York • San Francisco • New Haven, Conn • Waterville, Maine • London

Christine Nasso, *Publisher*
Elizabeth Des Chenes, *Managing Editor*

© 2010 Greenhaven Press, a part of Gale, Cengage Learning

For more information, contact:
Greenhaven Press
27500 Drake Rd.
Farmington Hills, MI 48331-3535
Or you can visit our Internet site at gale.cengage.com

LIBRARY OF CONGRESS CATALOGING-IN-PUBLICATION DATA

Performance-enhancing drugs / Tamara L. Roleff, book editor.
   p. cm. -- (Issues that concern you)
  Includes bibliographical references and index.
  ISBN 978-0-7377-4745-4 (hardcover)
 1. Doping in sports--Popular works. 2. Steroids Popular works. I.
Roleff, Tamara L., 1959-
  RC1230.P4763 2010
  362.29--dc22
                                                                    2009042493

Printed in the United States of America
 2 3 4 5 6 7 13 12 11 10

CONTENTS

In May 2009 Manny Ramirez, a baseball player for the Los Angeles Dodgers, was suspended for fifty games by Major League Baseball (MLB) for a violation of the league's drug policy. It was later revealed that Ramirez, who is one of the few ballplayers to hit more than five hundred home runs in his big league career (of which twenty were grand slams), had a prescription for human chorionic gonadotropin (HCG), a female fertility drug. While HCG is not a steroid or a performance-enhancing drug, it is used in combination with anabolic-androgenic steroids and is therefore banned by Major League Baseball. Steroids suppress the body's natural production of testosterone; HCG boosts the body to start testosterone production again.

In the two months following his suspension, Manny Ramirez never admitted to using steroids or any performance-enhancing substance. Sportswriters pressed him for information about his steroid use, but he refused to discuss it, saying only, "I didn't kill nobody, I didn't rape nobody, so that's it, I'm just going to come and play the game."[1] Ten days before his fifty-game suspension was up, MLB allowed Ramirez to start playing baseball in the minor leagues to get back into shape before going back to the major leagues again. When his name was announced prior to the start of his first minor-league game—forty-two games into his suspension—many of the fans stood and cheered. Dodgers manager Joe Torre defended the MLB rule that allowed Ramirez to play in the minor leagues on a rehabilitation assignment before his fifty-game suspension was over. "Then you might as well make it a sixty-game suspension. You're going to have to practice somewhere."[2]

Many Dodger fans did not seem to think that his alleged steroid use was cheating or even care about his alleged use. The fans seemed to be more upset that the Dodgers would be without his power hitting. Fans who watched Ramirez play in a minor

In May 2009 Major League Baseball suspended Manny Ramirez for fifty games for his violations of league drug policy.

league game during his suspension were very supportive of him and felt that he was different from other baseball players who took steroids. "There is something about him that makes him different from Barry Bonds, Mark McGwire, Jose Canseco, all those guys," said Dodger fan Tony Cruz. "It's his personality. His personality overcomes all of his wrongdoings."[3] Another fan, Lizette Rivero, does not think boos are warranted. "Aren't they all on something?" she asked. "If we don't cheer for players who are on something, then we can't cheer for anybody."[4]

Not everyone thinks that athletes who use steroids should be cheered by their fans. Sportswriter Bill Plaschke argues that fans who continue to blindly support Ramirez are allowing him "to maintain his lavish lifestyle as a truth cheat"[5] because they have not demanded an explanation nor an apology from the Dodgers outfielder. In a May 31, 2009, column in the *Los Angeles Times* about the possibility of fans voting for Ramirez to play in the All-Star game, Plaschke writes, "If you vote for Manny Ramirez, you are endorsing his cheating." Some baseball fans agree with Plaschke. Dan Howard thinks those who support Ramirez have "warped logic." He asks if "it's OK to be a cheating drug user if you are charismatic, talented and interesting like Manny."[6] Another fan who agrees is David Cook, who writes, "Manny is a drug user, a cheat, and a liar. He is laughing in the faces of all Dodger fans. Manny should be traded, or better yet, fired from the Dodgers."[7]

As fans of professional baseball, football, and basketball debate whether athletes who use steroids to gain an advantage should be cheered or booed, fans of Olympic and amateur sports do not have that concern. Elite-level athletes (such as college athletes, Olympians, and those who compete in prestigious events such as the Tour de France bicycle race) are banned from their sport for up to two years for a first offense if they test positive for banned substances. They face a lifetime ban for a second offense. But few athletes test positive for performance-enhancing substances in those sports. In 2008 the U.S. Anti-Doping Agency, the laboratory that tests Olympic, college, and elite-level athletes, tested 7,690 American athletes and found only 25 violations of its anti-doping rules.

Manny Ramirez is one of the most recent—and most famous—athletes to confront the issue of using performance-enhancing drugs, but he is far from alone. Others who have been accused or suspected of or who have admitted taking the banned drugs during the past few years include athletic superstars, such as baseball players Alex Rodriguez, Barry Bonds, Sammy Sosa, Jose Canseco, and Ken Caminiti; football players Bill Romanowski, Shawne Merriman, Matt Lehr, and Shaun Rogers; and professional bicyclists Lance Armstrong and Floyd Landis. Few have been sanctioned for use of performance-enhancing drugs.

The controversy over whether the use of performance-enhancing drugs is cheating and whether the athletes who are caught using the banned substances should be booed or cheered encapsulates some of the main arguments of the issue. On the one hand are the fans who are thrilled with the results the drugs give the athletes, and

In July 2009, when Manny Ramirez returned from suspension, thirty-five thousand Dodger fans made the trip to San Diego either to boo him or, more likely, to cheer for him.

on the other are those who believe athletes who use steroids are cheating and should be banned from the sport. The articles in this volume present a wide range of opinions on the many controversies surrounding performance-enhancing drugs.

Notes

1. Quoted in Jim Peltz, "Dodgers Slugger Manny Ramirez Speaks but Says Little About Suspension," *Los Angeles Times*, June 10, 2009, p. C1.

2. Quoted in Bill Shaikin, "Mannywood Will Be Reinstated as Well," *Los Angeles Times*, June 26, 2009, p. C9.

3. Quoted in Bill Plaschke, "SoCal Really Lets Manny Have It . . . with Love," *Los Angeles Times*, June 28, 2009, p. C1.

4. Quoted in Plaschke, "SoCal Really Lets Manny Have It," p. C1.

5. Bill Plaschke, "In a State of Suspended Disbelief over Manny Ramirez," *Los Angeles Times*, May 31, 2009, p. C1.

6. Quoted in T.J. Simers, "They're Crying Foul over Apologist for Manny Ramirez," *Los Angeles Times*, June 25, 2009, p. C3.

7. Quoted in Simers, "They're Crying Foul," p. C3.

ONE

Anabolic Steroids Are Dangerous Drugs

Dan Clark

Dan Clark, a former football player for the Los Angeles Rams, used steroids while he portrayed the wrestler Nitro on the popular reality TV series *American Gladiators*. In the following viewpoint Clark argues that steroids are dangerous drugs with harmful side effects. He asserts that users often experience out-of-control rages while taking steroids, and the violent tendencies often continue even after the users stop taking the drugs. According to Clark, athletes who take steroids tend to get injured more often and more severely, and he claims that the deaths of many athletes can also be blamed on steroids. In addition, Clark maintains that steroids are often a gateway drug to other illegal drugs.

No one wants to hear the truth about steroids before he or she takes them. I didn't. Despite all the negative information that's available, young athletes are still embracing steroids with a passion. It's easy to understand why. All teenagers are thinking about is improved performance and unlimited success—gold medals, home runs, touchdowns, a place in history. They don't want to know about breast tissue growing beneath their pectoral muscles, infertility, liver failure, brain cancer, or sexual dysfunction. They don't want to hear about the anger either—the uncontrollable and sudden bouts of 'roid rage.

An Ocean of Lies

We also need to wade through the *ocean of lies* told by some current steroid abusers to justify their usage. One of the biggest lies steroid users tell is *there is no such thing as 'roid rage.* I've heard a lot of chatter saying, "If you're a jerk before steroids, you'll be an even bigger jerk on steroids. But if you weren't, then you won't have a problem when you're on them." This is simply not true. . . . I have a scar that slices down from under my nose to the top of my upper lip that prompts some people to ask if I had a cleft lip as a child. I have another beauty under my bottom lip, too, and one that splays across the underside of my chin; not to mention two scars under my left eye and a nose that's been broken enough times that people assume I'm a professional boxer.

I wasn't the only one who got into fights. I've witnessed countless other incidents when guys were on the juice. I've seen fifty-pound dumbbells thrown across the gym and heads rammed through wooden doors. I watched a juicer friend of mine rip a guy out of a car through the window simply because the guy cut him off on the road. I've seen a fellow Gladiator, who at five feet ten tipped the scales with 285 pounds of ripped muscle, pick a guy up off the ground by the neck and slam him just because the guy stepped on his shoe. I also remember an incident in college when two of our biggest and strongest linemen, both weighing close to three hundred pounds, showed up at practice with their faces bruised and bludgeoned after getting into a fight with each other, even though they were best friends.

The Tip of the Iceberg

Fighting and smashing heads through windows is just the tip of the iceberg when it comes to 'roid rage. It goes miles deeper. An unusual number of bodybuilders (the ultimate steroid abusers) are behind bars for homicide.

The author, a former wrestler, says that athletes on steroids cannot avoid rages. He points to pictured wrestler Chris Benoit, who murdered his wife and child before taking his own life, as proof of the dangers of using performance-enhancing drugs.

Bertil Fox, a former Mr. World, is incarcerated for the murders of his girlfriend and his girlfriend's mother.

Southern California bodybuilder John Riccardi awaits execution for a double homicide.

Another California muscleman, Gordon Kimbrough, is serving twenty-seven years to life for the murder of his fiancée.

Former police officer and hard-core bodybuilder James Batsel is serving a life sentence for murder, shooting his victim nine times.

A female strength prodigy, Sally McNeil, is also serving life for the murder of her bodybuilder husband.

Bodybuilders are not the only offenders. Anyone who uses steroids is prone to homicidal rage. When professional wrestler Chris Benoit tragically strangled his wife and suffocated his seven-year-old son, then hung himself on June 25, 2007, his long-term use of steroids came to light.

Psychiatrist Harrison Pope of McLean Hospital in Massachusetts sometimes serves as an expert witness in court. He claims to have been involved in a dozen murder cases where someone using steroids—despite no previous history of violence or a criminal record—killed somebody. In one case, a sixteen-year-old boy was charged with killing his fourteen-year-old girlfriend. Pope says, "We have no evidence of any criminal or violent activity before he started taking steroids. At that point, he had a series of run-ins with the police, which culminated in the murder."

Damaged Wiring in the Brain

Another steroid lie: *once you get off the juice, the aggression disappears*. Not so, according to a recent study at Northeastern University. Long after more than one hundred hamsters were taken off steroids, the aggressive tendencies continued in 85 percent of them. Autopsies revealed steroids actually damaged the hamsters' brains. Even after steroids were discontinued, their anterior hypothalamus, known to regulate aggression, continued to pump out more of a neurotransmitter called vasopressin, which induces aggression.

Maybe this is why I still feel the fire of competition boiling in my blood and why a part of me will always miss hitting someone, will always miss the violence. I used to believe I was just wired this way. Now I suspect I've damaged the wiring in my brain with steroids.

One of the most insidious lies is *steroids help athletes recover from injuries more quickly*. The opposite is actually true. Injuries increase when on steroids. Look at baseball in the steroid era between 1992 and 2001. According to baseball doctor Bill Wilder in *ESPN the Magazine*, "The number of players on the DL [disabled list] rose from 352 to 465, a 32% increase. Days spent on the DL went from 17,920 to 27,779." Players were also hurt more severely. Days spent on the DL per injury increased 55 percent over that span. And injuries that were rarely problems before all the bulking up were now common: patellar tendonitis, strained rib cages, torn hamstrings—the kind of stuff that happens when oversize muscles rip away from bones that can no longer support them. The kind of stuff that happened to me when I tore my hamstring.

The Biggest Lie of All

The biggest steroids lie of all? *Steroids don't kill.*

Maybe we should ask Lyle Alzado. Or professional wrestlers Eddie Guerrero, Curt "Mr. Perfect" Henning, Ravishing Rick Rude, British Bulldog Davey Boy Smith. Ask bodybuilders Mohammed Benaziza and Andreas Münzer, who both competed in the Arnold Classic. Ask seventeen-year-old Taylor Hooton, a baseball player from Plano, Texas, or twenty-four-year-old baseball player Rob Garibaldi, who both committed suicide due to depression brought on by steroids. Or maybe we should ask my good friend and SAE [Sigma Alpha Epsilon] fraternity brother from San Jose State Ken Caminiti, the three-time All-Star and 1996 National League MVP [most valuable player]. Or better yet, let's ask famous steroid guru Dan Duchaine, who wrote the extremely popular *Underground Steroid Handbook*, a book that became the bible for those wanting to use steroids, who died an untimely death in 2000 at age forty-eight from complications of kidney disease. The question that begs to be answered, if he was so smart and knew how to take steroids safely, why is he dead?

These deaths captured the public's attention because the victims were high-profile people. I know that we'll never hear about countless other deaths attributed to steroid use. Yet, even in the face of these tragic deaths, pro-steroid pundits still deny the connection. They'll say Alzado died of a brain tumor, there's no

Side Effects from Steroid Abuse

Men	Women
• Shrinking of testicles	• Growth of facial hair
• Reduced sperm count	• Male-pattern baldness
• Infertility	• Deepened voice
• Baldness	• Changes in or cessation of menstrual cycle
• Development of breasts	• Enlargement of the clitoris
• Increased risk of prostate cancer	

Taken from: National Institute on Drug Abuse, *Steroids (Anabolic Androgenic)*, June 2008.

correlation. Caminiti was on painkillers. This bodybuilder died of dehydration, that wrestler died from something else. But the sobering truth is the one thread that ties all the deaths together is *steroids*.

A Gateway Drug

Over the years I've also learned steroids are a *gateway* to other psychotropic drugs. After you've crossed the line and taken an illegal drug, it's a lot easier to say yes to a line of blow, a tab of ecstasy, or a puff off a joint. You've already taken drugs to alter the way you feel. What's one more? On second thought, steroids are more than a gateway; they are an expressway to abuse. On steroids your motor is going so fast, and you've got so much energy and aggression gunning through your system, you've got to find a way to release it. I'll go even further and say I don't know a juicer who hasn't tried or doesn't use other illegal drugs.

Athletes Are Role Models

More than anything else, parents need to know how to deal with the subject of steroids with their children. I agree wholeheartedly with the leading recommendation of most rational antidrug campaigns. Talk to your kids often and early about steroids. If not, you're leaving their education in the hands of someone else. One of the biggest problems is that a kid sees Barry Bonds. He's forty-four. To a sixteen-year-old, that's more than a lifetime from now. I once heard a kid say, "I'm seventeen years old; forty-four is an old man. I don't care if I'm dead then." This shortsighted thinking makes it difficult for parents and puts the challenge square on the shoulders of the powers-that-be to stop drug use at the highest levels. We can't ask our children to avoid steroids if the athletes they admire use them with impunity.

No matter what anyone says, like it or not, professional athletes are role models and are setting the bar for younger kids. The trickle-down effect is immeasurable. As U.S. surgeon general Richard Carmona told the press, the problem of steroid use is "less a moral and ethical issue than it is a public health issue. If youngsters are seeing their role models practicing this kind of behavior and it seems acceptable, then we need to do something about that because it is a health risk." This is why it's crucial we stop steroid use in pro sports. Nothing less than our children's health is at stake.

Children Are Not Safe

And parents shouldn't think their children are safe because they aren't into sports. Recent studies show that teenagers use steroids to change their physical appearance, and alarmingly, the segment of the population with the fastest growth in taking steroids is teenage girls. The Centers for Disease Control estimates that around 7 percent of high school girls have tried steroids.

Dr. Charles Yesalis, a retired Penn State professor and a recognized authority on steroids, estimates that "at least half a million and probably closer to three-quarters of a million children in this country have used these drugs in their lifetime." Adds Yesalis,

"The teens I've talked to say [steroids and the human growth hormone, or HGH] are as easy to get as marijuana." The Mayo Clinic has published information that one-tenth of U.S. steroid users are teenagers.

Another major concern about kids and steroids is the manner in which the youngsters procure the drugs. Because sales of steroids and growth hormone have been pushed underground, kids are buying them off the Internet or from some gym junkie. The drugs they're getting are the rejected veterinary crap and the imported garbage from Mexico. If these kids were using the best stuff, that would be bad enough, but it's worse because they're using the terrible, toxic stuff. . . .

Sickened and Appalled

With all of the overwhelming information on the toxicity of anabolic steroids, I'm amazed and sickened that some people out there, such as Jose Canseco, still advocate the use of steroids. I'm appalled and frightened when I consider the effects that his popular book *Juiced* have had on the American psyche, particularly that of the younger generation.

The eyes of the world are focused on this. It's up to us to pull together as a nation and conquer the steroid crisis that is crippling sports and our society. We now know the extent of the problem. Everyone is culpable. No one can look the other way. Through the telling of my story, I hope that my experience will discourage others from taking the dangerous and destructive steroid route. Just as Nitro pioneered a unique and powerful kind of physical fitness and confidence, I hope that with this book Dan Clark will lead others away from becoming victimized by a cycle that will destroy their health and happiness. We've all felt the effects of the cycle. Now it's up to us to save today's youth from sacrificing an entire life so as to become a hero for less than fifteen minutes of fame.

TWO

Steroid Drugs Are Not All Bad

Gary Cartwright

> The Mitchell Report is Major League Baseball's report on performance-enhancing drug use in baseball. According to journalist Gary Cartwright, the report unintentionally exposes the myths of steroid abuse. He contends that steroids are not responsible for destroying the integrity of the game; the owners who thumb their noses at the public are doing a fine job on their own, he writes. Nor does he believe that steroid use turns athletes into freaks since athletes have above-average abilities in the first place; steroids just make the users easier to identify. According to Cartwright, not all steroids are dangerous. He concludes that steroids should be controlled, not banned.

The holy warriors of the anti-doping crusade have achieved the near-impossible: They have made me feel sorry for Roger Clemens. When [former U.S. senator] George Mitchell's report on the use of performance-enhancing drugs in baseball, requested by commissioner Bud Selig, made Clemens its poster boy, the reputation of one of the best pitchers the game has witnessed was instantly destroyed. The allegations were based almost entirely on the testimony of Clemens's former personal trainer, Brian McNamee, who was threatened with prosecution if he lied to

Gary Cartwright, "Truth and Consequences," *Texas Monthly*, vol. 36, April, 2008, pp. 82–85. Copyright 2008 Texas Monthly, Inc. Reproduced by permission.

Mitchell's investigators. That's what the crusaders were waiting for, a big name, someone less odious than, say, Barry Bonds. We may learn the truth from the upcoming FBI investigation into whether Clemens committed perjury, or the conflict between Clemens and his accusers may remain unresolved, but either way, the damage is done. "Mitchell has thrown a skunk in the jury box," Rusty Hardin, Clemens's Houston-based attorney, told me. "Whatever happens now, we'll never be able to remove the smell."

A Shadow of Suspicion

A shadow of suspicion has trailed Clemens since October 2006, when the *Los Angeles Times* reported that an affidavit for a search warrant, sworn to by a federal investigator, fingered McNamee,

Roger Clemens testifies at a hearing before the U.S. House of Representatives Committee on Oversight and Government Reform for the Mitchell Report, denying allegations that he used steroids.

Clemens, and several other players in a performance-enhancer drug case. Clemens steadfastly denied using performance enhancers (and, indeed, fourteen months later, the *Times* ran a correction saying that he had not been named in the affidavit after all). He repeated those denials after the Mitchell report appeared in December [2007], first in an interview with Mike Wallace on *60 Minutes*, in which he admitted to taking injections of vitamin B_{12} and the painkiller lidocaine but angrily rejected McNamee's contentions that he'd received steroids and human growth hormone (HGH), then in a press conference so packed with self-righteous indignation that he stormed off the stage when the questions got too sticky.

To rebut allegations that Clemens's career rebounded about the time he supposedly first started using performance enhancers, his agent, Randy Hendricks, released an 18,000-word report, com-

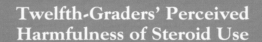

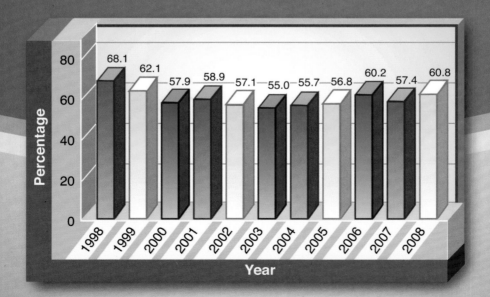

Taken from: Monitoring the Future Survey. www.monitoringthefuture.org/data/08data/pr08t7pdf.

plete with statistics, maintaining that his remarkable longevity (Clemens is 45) was due to his ability to adjust his pitching style. To compensate for a decrease in the velocity of his fastball, which had been his trademark since he broke in with the Boston Red Sox, in 1983, Clemens, the report said, utilized a split-finger fastball. Indeed, he won the fourth of his seven Cy Young awards in 1997, at age 35, a year after the Red Sox decided he was washed-up and a year before McNamee claims that Clemens started using steroids.

On February 13, Clemens went to Capitol Hill to repeat his denials, this time under oath. The House Committee on Oversight and Government Reform had all but commanded his appearance, because he had dared to challenge the Mitchell report. "How did we reach the stage where a guy is criticized for publicly denying guilt?" Hardin asks. Clemens hasn't been charged with a crime, but the court of public opinion has already rendered its guilty verdict.

Our Newest National Hysteria

It's almost as though the holy warriors were waiting for a star of Clemens's magnitude to make it official that performance enhancers are our newest national hysteria, nudging aside old standbys like bird flu, sharks, and red hordes [Communists]. This has gone beyond silly. Who among us hasn't used performance enhancers, preferably with ice and an olive? Steroids, synthetic substances similar to testosterone, can be as benign as those that are commonly prescribed for allergies and as harmful as those that have sent many retired athletes into physical decline; as with any medication, the effect depends on the dose and frequency of use. Anabolic steroids, the type that bulk up muscles, are used to treat certain kinds of anemia and offset the loss of testosterone caused by aging. I've taken them and regularly use a steroid nasal spray. My dog Allie takes steroid shots for her hot spots. Another type of steroid, called a corticosteroid, is used to reduce swelling. The real question ought to focus on intent: If an athlete uses steroids to change his body, as Barry Bonds apparently did, the public has every reason to be outraged. If an athlete uses them to combat aging, so what?

All steroids enhance performance and, if misused, can cause trouble. There have been a few cases where the premature death of an athlete was possibly the result of steroid use, most notably those involving Lyle Alzado, a defensive end for the Denver Broncos, who believed that steroids were the cause of his fatal brain lymphoma, and Houston Astros and San Diego Padres slugger Ken Caminiti, a user of cocaine and steroids who died of a heart attack at 41.

Anything for an Advantage

For the most part, however, the only thing certifiably bad about steroids is that they may improve athletic performance. Somehow we've decided that the only hardworking professionals who shouldn't be permitted to enhance their performances are athletes. Amphetamines were staples in professional training rooms in the sixties and seventies—Jim Bouton's book *Ball Four*, published in 1970, is full of talk about popping "greenies"—and are still widely used. "Amphetamines are the real performance-enhancing drugs that people should always have been worried about," Allan Lans, the New York Mets' team psychiatrist from 1987 to 2003, told the *New York Times*. The mind-set of the elite athlete is, do anything it takes to get an advantage. Athletes training for the Beijing Olympics have asked the physiologist for the U.S. Olympic Committee if they should acclimate themselves to the city's dreadful pollution by running behind buses and breathing the exhaust. In his *60 Minutes* interview Clemens cheerfully admitted that until the painkiller Vioxx was taken off the market, he gobbled it "like it was Skittles." . . .

Baseball Myths

Its rush to judgment aside, the Mitchell report may have performed a public service by shooting holes in some of baseball's more suspect myths. Start with the illusion that drugs are destroying the integrity of the game. Integrity? Oh, you mean like the monopoly that Congress gives owners, granting them an exemption from antitrust laws and allowing them to thumb their noses at the public while juiced-up stars such as Mark McGwire and Bonds smash the game's most cherished home run records? You might say the real victims of steroids are Hank Aaron and Babe Ruth. Meanwhile, owners bulk up on steroids without having to actually take the nasty things. Baseball revenues soared as home run records fell, jumping from $2.9 billion in 1998 to just over $6 billion last year.

Then there is the myth that steroids are turning players into freaks. Players have always been freaks. That's what makes them so different from the rest of us. No normal person can throw a baseball 98 miles an hour. Normal people can't run a slant-in and catch a football with a 250-pound linebacker waiting to cream them. Baseball is no more egregious than professional football, but cheaters are easier to identify because baseball is a game intoxicated with statistics, such as Clemens's 354 career wins or Bonds's 762 career home runs.

Control, Not Ban

It is time to admit that not all steroids are dangerous and that every individual and every situation cannot be addressed with the same set of rigid rules. Instead of banning steroids, we should control them. Cool the hysteria; educate without scaring. Understand the problem. "There is a tipping point in a player's career where he goes from chasing the dream to running from a nightmare," former big-league outfielder Doug Glanville wrote recently in an essay published in the *New York Times*' op-ed page. "At that point, ambition is replaced with anxiety, passion is replaced with survival." If an athlete like Clemens needs medication to overcome the aches and pains of aging and the fear of failure—if he needs a little help to keep on keeping on—whose business is it, anyway?

Granted, the use of performance enhancers sends a bad message to young people, but so do a lot of other things, like drinking and smoking. Hasn't our collective experience taught us that prohibition doesn't work and that we can't totally kid-proof society? A larger problem with liberalizing the use of steroids is that players who want to compete might be forced to use them against their wishes. That happens, beyond a doubt. We need to make a distinction, as previous generations did, between amateurs and professionals. Sports on an elite level is an inherently unhealthy pursuit; professionals define themselves by what they are willing to do to succeed. *Washington Post* sports columnist Sally Jenkins has written that "world-class athletes are in the business of torturing their bodies unnaturally," of changing the body's chemistry and pushing it to unnatural extremes. It's the price they have agreed to pay.

So let's give poor Roger Clemens a break. He's not a drug addict or even a serious abuser. In the four-year span that McNamee claims to have juiced Clemens, he took a total of maybe sixteen injections—hardly enough to account for a career of greatness or do any harm to the game. Now he faces a perjury investigation that comes down to his word against his accusers'. It seems as if Roger Clemens is being prosecuted not just because he may have used steroids but because he acted like a jerk.

THREE

Using Performance-Enhancing Drugs Is Cheating

Richard W. Pound

> Richard W. Pound is the founder and former chair of the World Anti-Doping Agency (WADA), an independent organization created in 1999 to fight doping in sporting competitions. He believes that rules are a fundamental and elemental part of sports. Pound maintains that everyone who plays in games and sports must agree to abide by the established rules. According to Pound, one of the rules in national and international sports competitions is that doping—using performance-enhancing drugs—is prohibited. Therefore, he argues, anyone who uses a prohibited drug is cheating.

Sport is part of the games-playing matrix that is peculiar to humans. A lot of animals like to play, but human beings seem to be hardwired for game-playing. It is a fundamental characteristic of the human race.

If, at this moment, all our memories were wiped out and we had no recollection whatsoever of any game or sport, it would probably be a matter of hours before someone would pick up a stone and throw it at another object to see if he could hit it. Or try to run faster than someone else. Or hit an object with a stick.

Or lift a heavy weight. Others would try to follow suit to see who could hit closest to the target, run the fastest, bash the object the farthest, lift the heaviest weight.

Before long, we would agree on rules about how each challenge would be attempted, what was OK and what was not. Games would be developed, with a series of established rules and regulations for each. Someone would eventually write the rules and regulations down so that everyone would know how the game was to be played. Others would agree to act as referees in order to make sure that everyone followed the rules. Competitions would spring up between individuals and groups and, in time, we would get back to where we are right now—with a complex international sports system, involving hundreds of millions of athletes and even more spectators. There would, in all likelihood, be an astonishing similarity to the essential elements of what we now know as sports and games. OK, maybe not cricket or real tennis, but many of the sports we now enjoy.

Rules Are Important

One of the most important elements of sport is that the participants agree on the rules. Think about it: without the rules, there would be no games. In many respects, these rules are artificial, occasionally arbitrary, but that is not the point. The point is that they are the rules of the game and, furthermore, that they are rules upon which the participants have agreed. If you are competing against me in a game, I expect that you will follow the rules. You are entitled to the same expectations of me.

If all of us who play the game agree to change the rules, for whatever reason, that's fine, but, until we do, neither of us can unilaterally change them. If in the shotput, we decide that the shot will weigh sixteen pounds, I cannot hollow out mine and compete with a twelve-pound shot just because I am not as strong as you, or because your technique is more effective than mine and I need something to "level the playing field" in my eyes. I cannot play hockey with a bigger curve in the stick or use a corked bat in baseball. I can't start a race before the official signal or run only eleven laps instead of the required twelve. And so on.

The rules are, if you like, our social contract with each other. That's our deal. In society in general, you may be governed by laws with which you may not agree or in which you had no say, but in sport, you always have a choice. If you do not agree with the rules, you do not have to participate. It's quite simple. You are in, or you are out. I'm not going to offer any moral judgment regarding someone who opts out. That is a free choice and a matter of individual decision. But if someone pretends to accept the rules and then cheats, that's something else entirely.

Today, there are lots of rules. Some of them are technical, such as for equipment, size of playing fields, number of players and measurement of success or winning. Some are safety-driven, such as helmets or padding for skiers, hockey players and boxers. Some are designed to protect health, such as minimum ages for competitors, weight categories, medical examinations and safety nets. And so it goes. This is what we buy into when we participate in sport. We promise to play by the rules. It is our ethical commitment, to ourselves and to our opponents and to any spectators who may watch us play. . . .

Doping

One of the rules in national and international sport is that doping is prohibited. Doping is the international term that refers to the use of performance-enhancing substances or methods. The original anti-doping rules were adopted out of concerns for the health and safety of the athletes. But, while we're obviously still very much concerned with the health of the athletes, the rules have evolved to protect the ethics underlying sport.

The prohibited substances and methods of doping have varied over time with the expansion of scientific knowledge. A few have been removed from the list of prohibited substances and methods or reclassified for purposes of further study. Others have been added as scientists have become aware of the effects and side effects of their use. What is on or off the list from time to time is not particularly important from a conceptual perspective. What *is* important is that we all agree that we will not use or do the things that are on the list. That, as I have said, is our deal with each other. Our promise to each other.

The Sociopaths of Sport

We are not perfect, though, and there are those who are quite willing to ignore rules to get an unfair advantage over their competitors. Cheaters are the sociopaths of sport, who care nothing for their own promises, who do not respect their fellow competitors, who do not respect the game they are playing and who, in the end, do not even respect themselves. All that matters to them is winning at any cost, and they are willing to cheat or willing to be persuaded to cheat in order to win.

Based on my experience in the field, I have concluded that, in most cases, it is not athletes acting alone. They are assisted, counseled, sometimes tricked and occasionally forced into cheating. Coaches, trainers, medical doctors, scientists, sports administrators, agents, international or national sports federations, national Olympic committees and even some misguided parents (all of whom know better or who have a professional or moral responsibility to the young people under their charge) conspire to destroy the value of what the athletes are trying to do. Some of the worst offenders in the past have been governments, whose distorted sense of national pride has led them to achieve results by organized cheating.

Why should athletes . . . be forced into the downward cycle of the lowest common denominator simply because there are some who are willing to cheat, with all of the risks of disgrace and health problems that may follow? There is an easy answer to this question. They should not.

And here is where the need to ensure a level playing field comes in. Someone must act to protect those who play fair. It is important to develop a culture focused on the prevention of cheating, creating a new mind-set and helping everyone involved to understand the reasons why there should be no cheating. It is also important to be realistic. In society, there will always be those who act outside the law, which is why we have police forces, court systems and specified punishments for breaking the law. It would be foolish to think that similar mechanisms are not required in sport. . . .

Officials, Doctors, and Coaches

The officials who cheat make a mockery of their responsibilities and trivialize the years of training and dedication of the trusting athletes whom they betray. A notorious example of corrupt

At the 2002 Salt Lake City Olympics, Canadian skaters Jamie Salé and David Pelletier were denied a gold medal because corrupt French and Russian officials conspired to fix the results of their competition.

judging occurred at the Salt Lake City Olympic Winter Games in 2002, when French and Russian officials conspired to fix the results in the pairs figure skating event. Canadians Jamie Salé and David Pelletier were betrayed by figure skating officials and judges who were fixing results to further personal ambitions. This happens all too often, and not just in figure skating.

Medical doctors and scientists conspire to assist athletes and others to cheat by developing and administering performance-enhancing drugs. They know that what they are doing is against

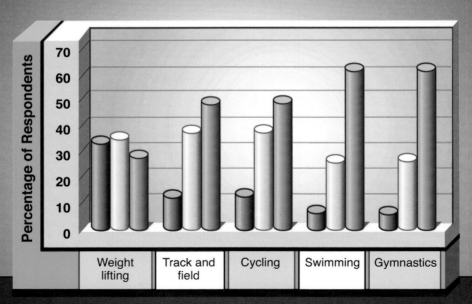

Fans Believe Few Olympians Use Performance-Enhancing Drugs

A nationwide survey found that Americans believe that only a few Olympic athletes use performance-enhancing drugs.

People were asked to estimate how many Olympic athletes use performance-enhancing drugs:

■ All or most   ■ Some   ■ Ony a few or none

Taken from: USA Today/Gallup Poll, July 25–27, 2008.

the rules of sport and that the drugs are potentially harmful to the athletes who use them. In many cases, the side effects are little known, yet they risk the health of athletes because they want to win. The designer steroid THG went directly from the laboratory into the systems of athlete users. The Hippocratic oath, sworn by all medical doctors, includes the undertaking to do no harm. Do no harm, indeed!

And as for coaches, in my view, there is no coach worthy of the description who can be unaware of drug use by athletes under her or his care. It is a responsibility of coaches to develop—and not to destroy—the health and character of those under their care. I do not want my children or grandchildren under the influence of a coach willing to encourage or permit them to use drugs. The role of the coach is not simply to produce better athletic performance, but to develop the athlete as a complete human being. . . .

World Anti-Doping Agency

Technically, doping in sport is not a criminal activity (depending on the substances), but rather one that should be handled within the sport context, as a breach of a sport rule, and where necessary with the help of governments. The World Anti-Doping Agency [WADA] is attempting to level the playing field. It performs an absolutely independent role in trying to make sport doping-free. We bring together the sports movement and the governments of the world and put them at the same table, at the same time, with the same objective: to restore the integrity of sport by giving every athlete an equal chance of doing his or her best without having to cheat. . . .

Positive Guidance

Those of us in a position to help prepare our youth for useful roles in society have a duty to do whatever we can to ensure that our guidance is positive. To win their confidence, we need to show them that the values we talk about are the same values that we practice, support and protect for their benefit. It is a huge responsibility, particularly in a world that is struggling to find its way, and in which the remarkable pace of change has produced an unfortunate tendency to believe that whatever may come from the past is *passé* [outmoded] and of no value.

There is nothing *passé* about trying to do your best, within the limits we must all accept as members of civilized society, whether on the field of play in sport, or on the general field of play within society. There is nothing *passé* about ethical principles, about respect for yourself and for others. We should embrace the positive values of understanding who we are, doing what is morally right and rejecting what is morally wrong—not because someone else tells us to do so, but because we know personally, at the very center of our beings, what is right and what is wrong. Many years ago, Bishop Fulton Sheen expressed the idea in compelling terms: "Wrong is wrong, even if everybody is doing it, and right is right, even if nobody is doing it."

FOUR

Using Performance-Enhancing Drugs Is Not Cheating

Radley Balko

Radley Balko is a senior editor for *Reason* magazine who participated in a debate about using steroids in sports. Balko argues that the debate about steroids use in sports is not about fairness in competition, nor about the athletes' health. Neither is it about protecting children from the influence of drugs, he maintains. Balko contends that those who support banning steroids in sports do so out of paternalism and a desire for control. According to Balko, sport is about stretching the limits of human potential. If a drug can make someone a better athlete, then athletes should have the freedom to make that choice, he asserts.

On the train ride from [Washington] D.C. this morning, we passed through Baltimore. It reminded me of one of my favorite authors, Baltimore native H.L. Mencken, who I think would've had a good laugh at the hypocrisy, the posturing, and the moral prudery associated with the steroid controversy. Eighty years ago, Mencken aptly summarized this debate when he wrote, "The urge to save humanity is almost always a false-face for the urge to rule it."

Let me start by saying that I believe private sports organizations should be able to set their own rules, and that they should be free to discipline in any manner they see fit the players who break

Radley Balko, "Should We Allow Performance-Enhancing Drugs in Sports?" *Reason*, January 23, 2008. Reproduced by permission.

those rules. I don't think Congress should forcibly allow performance enhancing substances in sports any more than I think Congress should prohibit them.

That said, we're here today to debate what those rules ought to be.

Fairness and Competition?

So why exactly do people [want] to ban some substances from professional sports?

If it's about fairness and competition, I'm dubious. Take Rep. Tom Davis, one of the more camera-hungry politicians to demagogue [appeal to emotions and prejudices] this issue. After the 2000 census, Rep. Davis maneuvered to have his congressional district gerrymandered [to have the boundaries redrawn] to include as many Republicans as possible, ensuring his continual reelection, and limiting the number of real options for his constituents. He ran the next year unopposed. Davis also snuck a provision into an unrelated piece of federal legislation preventing an apartment complex from going up in his district because, he said, he feared it would bring too many Democrats into his district.

This guy is cheating at *democracy*, and he's lecturing baseball players about fairness.

It's hard to believe the steroid panic is really about the safety of our athletes, either. My copanelist [pediatrician and expert in medical ethics] Dr. Norman Fost I think has ably shown that the alleged side affects of anabolic steroids are overstated, and the negative side effects of HGH [human growth hormone] are negligible at best.

Health Risks?

If we want to talk about health risks and professional sports, we might discuss the ballooning, unrelated-to-steroids weight of NFL linemen over the last 20 years, and the corresponding drop in life expectancy that's come with it.

Or we might talk about the particularly hellish world of thoroughbred horseracing jockeys, who subject themselves to sweatboxes, diuretics and suppositories, and intentional eating disorders.

In fact, any world-class athlete subjects his body to stresses it wasn't really designed to endure.

As we've seen with government bans on consensual activity—from alcohol to gambling to cocaine to prostitution—prohibitions not only don't work, they make the activity in question more dangerous by pushing it underground.

For the Children?

So what about the children? As with just about every paternalistic policy dating back to alcohol prohibition, many a politician has iterated over the last few years that we need to ban performance enhancing drugs "for the children."

But survey data actually shows that teen steroid use has mirrored the use of other illicit drugs over the years. It went up mildly in the 1990s, and has since either dropped slightly or leveled off since 2000. It's likely that the same trends that govern cocaine or marijuana use govern teen steroid use far more than what's happening in the sports pages.

In fact, a study released last year [in 2007]—[one] of the few studies to attempt to find out what motivates teens to take steroids—found that the most reliable indicator of steroid use was a teen's own body image and self-esteem.

The suggestion—and I think we can all agree it's pretty intuitive—is that the teenage boys who do take steroids do so not because they want to look like Barry Bonds or Mark McGwire, but because they want to look good for teenage girls.

So what is this debate really all about?

Paternalism and Control

I'd submit it's about paternalism and control. A few luddites [people against advancement, especially technological progress] and prudes have successfully induced a full-blown moral panic over a set of substances that for whatever reason have attracted the ire

Sports Fans Do Not Suspect Steroid Use

When sports fans hear about an athlete breaking a world record, most are not suspicious that the athlete used performance-enhancing drugs.

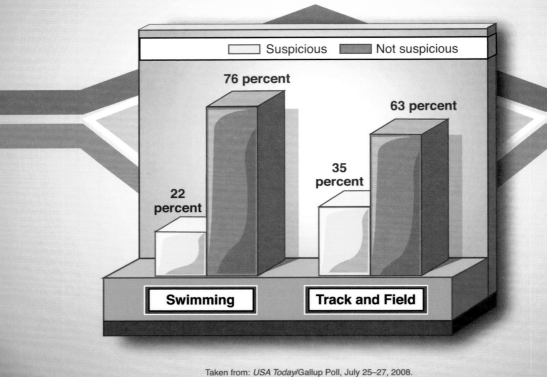

Taken from: *USA Today*/Gallup Poll, July 25–27, 2008.

of the people who have made it their job to tell us what is and isn't good for us.

Our society has an oddly schizophrenic relationship with pharmaceuticals and medical technology. If something can be said to be "natural," we tend to be okay with it. If it seems lab-made or synthetic we tend to be leery. But even synthetic drugs and manmade technology seem to be okay if the aim is to make sick or broken people whole again.

It's when we talk about expanding or transcending what we've come to consider "normal," be it through psychoactive drugs, performance-enhancing drugs, or genetic or biomedical technology, that a certain uneasiness sets in.

There was an article in the *Chronicle of Higher Education* last month [December 2007] about university professors taking stimulants like Adderall to increase their academic productivity. Oddly, the article quoted several professors who considered this "cheating" at academics. I have to confess, I don't understand this way of thinking. Academics is the search for truth and knowledge. If a drug can make that search more productive with few side effects, why in the world *wouldn't* you want to take it?

It's also important to note that we consider perfectly natural and acceptable today was quite out of the ordinary not so long ago. 100 years ago, life expectancy in the U.S. was 50 years of age. Today it's 78. Thanks to technology, medicine, and pharmaceuticals we are today taller, stronger, faster, healthier, and can expect to live longer than ever before. Genetically enhanced agriculture, anti-aging technology, and other advancements we've yet to see today—all of which seem as foreign to us now as penicillin likely seemed 50 years ago—will push our longevity even higher.

It's an old cliché that sports is a metaphor for the human condition. But there's a lot of truth to it. As technology helped humanity obliterate these milestones and move beyond what until 100 years ago had been a long, bleak history, similar advances in nutrition, training, and using technology to improve technique have enabled sports records to fall with astonishing regularity. Tennis players serve in excess of 120 mph [miles per hour]. Record times in the 100, 200, mile, and marathon continue to crumble.

Stretching the Limits

Sports is about exploring and stretching the limits of human potential. Going back even to the pre-modern Olympics, when athletes ate live bees and ate crushed sheep testicles to get a leg up on the competition, sports has never been some wholesome display of physical ability alone. Ingenuity, innovation, and knowledge about *what* makes us faster and stronger (and avoiding what might do more harm than good) has always been a part of the game.

It shouldn't be surprising, then, that many of the biggest proponents of banning performance enhancing drugs in sports are also suspect of continued advances in human achievement. Take Leon Kass, formerly President [George W.] Bush's top advisor on bioethics. The same Mr. Kass who champions rigorous drug testing in sports has also spent much of his career actually lamenting rising average human life expectancy, which he considers contrary to some odd concept of the natural order.

Of course there have been luddites and naturalists like Mr. Kass standing athwart the tide of human progress for much of recorded history. The essence of the disagreement today I think is that people like Mr. Kass and Mr. Richard Pound [founder of the World Anti-Doping Agency] have a decidedly different definition of what's pure, natural, and human than what I do.

For me, the essence of humanity is the pursuit of knowledge, and broadening and conquering the outer limits of our potential. For others, "human" by definition entails concrete limitations— it's more about adhering to and abiding by well-defined historical, cultural, moral, and philosophical concepts of personhood. I'd like to live to be 150. Leon Kass believes we should all be content with 75.

I think each of us ought to be free to choose and pursue our respective notions of humanity as we may. Let there be sports leagues that thrive on "pure sport," whatever that is, and let there be sports leagues where athletes are left to balance their own health and career longevity with technology, pharamacology, and the quest for a competitive advantage. If Mr. Kass wants to volunteer to be euthanized at 75, that's his prerogative. Me, I'll eagerly lap up what science can conjure—both to extend my life, and to better appreciate and enjoy it while I'm living it.

Knowing What Is Best for Society

Unfortunately many who take our opponents' position aren't content with merely holding to their own view of what's human

The author asserts that the debate over steroids is not about fairness in competition or the athletes' health but about control by the governing bodies of sport.

and what's acceptably "natural." They demand that the rest of us accept their concept of humanity, too. People like Mr. Pound and Mr. Kass want Congress and other government bodies to impose their will on society. Because they, better than we, know what's best for us.

Of course even if they're right and I'm wrong about the morality and propriety of some of these issues, a free society isn't really free at all if it doesn't include the freedom to make what some may believe are bad decisions.

Our opponents want to legislate away what they believe are the bad decisions. To borrow from H.L. Mencken, they believe they need to rule sports in order to save it.

FIVE

A Double Standard Applies to Performance Enhancements in Sports

Carl Thomen

In the following viewpoint Carl Thomen argues that to allow athletes to use technological innovations in their equipment and not inside their bodies is hypocritical. Improvements in design and materials of sports equipment and athletic wear have allowed athletes to play harder, longer, and faster than ever before, he asserts. According to the author, elite athletes possess qualities such as skill, judgment, and courage that are not affected by performance-enhancing drugs. He contends that using performance-enhancing drugs allows athletes to play at a level appropriate to their underlying ability. Thomen was a member of the South African National Championship–winning Eastern Province field hockey team in 2003 and has coached professionally both in South Africa and England. He is currently completing his PhD in athletic philosophy.

People are generally opposed to the use of performance enhancers, and this negative reaction has a number of arguments at its root. Critics claim that these drugs affect the purity of the sport, or that they could possibly have unforeseen and negative side-effects on athletes. By far the most prominent claim against

Carl Thomen, "Excerpts of Master Thesis Paper for Philosophy of Sports," *There Is a Double Standard Over Performance-Enhancing Drugs in Sport*, May 6, 2009. Reproduced by permission of the author.

performance enhancers is that they give an illegal and undeserved edge to those who use them.

Questioning the use of performance enhancers is valuable, as it leads to discussions concerning the legitimacy of rewarding athletes who are using all types of synthetic aids to be better and, ultimately, to win. There are also important ethical questions which occur on the slippery slope between sport in the traditional, amateur, 'Greek', understanding of the term, and sport played by super-enhanced, 'semi-human', and extremely well-paid athletes. If technology allowed one to alter one's genes, or to attach robotic arms, legs, etc. to become better at a sport (or for that matter, better human beings), should we allow it? Before considering the claim that performance enhancers give an athlete an undeserved and unfair edge, I would first like to consider responses to some standard positions on the use of performance enhancing drugs.

The Case for Performance-Enhancing Drugs

Celebrated British essayist Professor Lincoln Allison challenges the standard view that performance enhancing drugs should be banned from sport. First, Allison states that, for him at least, sport is valuable because it gives everyone the chance to participate, and because it allows us to watch and take sides as professionals exhibit those *non-physical* qualities that set them apart from others with possibly the same *physical* characteristics; qualities such as skill, tactical awareness, judgment, courage, vision, risk assessment and strategic thinking. Performance enhancing drugs do not, and could not, conceivably alter *these* qualities. Although there is no dispute that doping improves 'animal' attributes such as brute strength, power and stamina, Allison argues that if these attributes could be improved by doping, then all the better for the sport concerned, as athletes would be quicker, able to jump higher, lift heavier weights and last longer on the field of play. As Allison puts it, an athlete who uses performance enhancing drugs just "moves up to the level appropriate to her underlying ability".

Second, Allison questions the assumption that doping will have a negative effect on the spectator; that people would be put off watching a sport if they knew that performance enhancers were used. He considers a few famous contemporary cases. When an inquiry into the Tour de France found widespread use of EPO drugs[1] the supporters didn't care. A full house was present to watch Mark McGwire break Major League Baseball's homerun record, even though it was common knowledge that he used the performance enhancer nandrolone. Finally, Allison asks whether the fact that the number of players in the NFL [National Football League] that weigh over 140kg [308 lbs.] has skyrocketed from 10 a couple of years ago, to over 300 today, is simply because of high protein diets? So, if doping does not influence what we really value in sports prowess, and, if as a matter of fact, spectators don't care, then why not allow it?

Allison's argument is strong; I would now like to consider the claim that performance enhancers give an athlete an undeserved and unfair edge in competition. By doing so I would like to draw attention to the inherent double standards displayed in the official attitudes towards doping and technology. The fact is, we allow performance enhancers already. It's just that we keep them outside our bodies. Consider the following:

Improved Equipment

As recently as the early nineties, field hockey goalkeepers wore pads made of sponge rubber and cane, gloves similar to those of a cricket batsman, and only the most rudimentary face protectors and helmets. Nowadays, wearing a kit like that would be suicide. Why? Has the game of hockey changed so that it is easier to make circle entries and shoot for goal? Are there new techniques that put keepers at a disadvantage and make them more vulnerable? On the contrary, provisions have been made (especially in set pieces like the penalty corner) that make it harder to score. These include making it compulsory for the ball to leave the circle— the shooting area—before it is allowed to be returned for a shot on goal. The simple answer to the question of why goalkeepers need so much more protection, and why rules such as the above

1. Erythropoietin (EPO) increases oxygen uptake and therefore energy.

The author considers the use of new sports equipment technologies that enhance an athlete's performance—like the high-tech materials now used in hockey sticks—to be no different from using performance-enhancing drugs.

have been introduced, can be summed up in two words: the stick. Hockey sticks have developed from long pieces of curved yellow-wood, in a shape similar to that of a flat banana, into potentially lethal weapons. Not one member of the current South African national hockey side uses a wooden stick. They use sticks made of a combination of graphite, aramide, kevlar and carbon fibre. Why? Because sticks like these enable one to literally hit the cover off a ball. Ten years ago, that would have been unthinkable. However, the evolution doesn't end there. Sticks are now geometrically curved in a nature similar to that of a hunting bow. This enables anyone wanting to flick the ball (lifting the ball by slinging it along the stick) to do so with much more power, as the ball gathers more momentum as it travels across the length of the stick. Because of this, the drag-flick from a penalty corner is now a standard option, and allows teams to score more goals. International teams such as Pakistan, Germany and Holland have perfected it to such an extent that they don't need any other variations to score since their players can flick a ball at the same speed as they can hit it. Perhaps the reader should stop and consider that fact, and its implications for the goalkeeper and the defending players. First, these improvements have meant that defending teams have had to put more emphasis on safety: face masks and groin and hand protection have become mandatory. Second, with improvements such as these, it is getting exponentially harder to stop the opposition from scoring.

Technological Improvements

Technological innovations such as the above are present in all sports, and at all levels. Companies like Nike, Adidas, Speedo, New Balance and Reebok are constantly striving to manufacture products which give athletes the edge over their opponents. One just has to take a look at the sportswear on show at the recent Olympic Games in Beijing to realize this. For example, swimmers are now using full-body suits made out of material that minimizes friction with the water. Yes, would come the reply, but how much difference do these suits really make? The answer is simple: Even if they shave hundredths of a second off a swimmers time, they have done their job, as it is a fact that swimming is a sport where split seconds do matter.

Track athletes are also wearing ever more technologically improved outfits. When Cathy Freeman won the 400 metres at the Sydney Olympics, she was wearing a full-body Nike 'Windsuit', designed, as far-fetched as it may sound, to reduce air friction and thus make her run faster. Spiked athletic shoes are also standard issue today. These shoes have been proved to reduce times by full seconds by virtue of the better grip, and therefore propulsion, that they afford the athlete. Simply put, if you don't wear them, you are going to lose. It is the impact of these and other technologies on sport that Kalevi Heinila has in mind when he refers to the process of "totalization" in sport. Heinila argues that competitions now have a 'hidden validity'—they have ceased to be about the athletes themselves. What are competing now, instead, are total systems of human, economic, scientific and technological resources. Sigmund Loland, paraphrasing Heinila, states that he is "talking [here] about everything from scientifically regulated training and diet programs and nutritional supplements to the use of drugs, and in the future, genetic technologies."

The immediate response to this argument is to say that technological enhancements do indeed improve performance, but that they do not do so in the unfair (and illegal) manner of performance-enhancing drugs. After all, aren't hockey sticks and swimming suits available to everyone? The case of Italian swimmer Filippo Magnini and Speedo's LZR racer would, however, seem to refute this idea. Magnini was willing to risk a substantial fine from Italian swimming team sponsors Arena in order to wear the faster LZR racing suit, saying that in the LZR, "Mediocre swimmers suddenly become Martians". This statement echoes the words of Australian Libby Lenton, who said the suit made her feel as if she was "swimming downhill". It is simply the case that if you are sponsored by Speedo rather than Arena or Mizuno, or for that matter happen to live in a technologically advanced country, your performances will be better than those who are not sponsored by Speedo (or at all), or who happen to live in a Third World country. Is that fair?

Super Athletes

The examples above of swimmers and track athletes are particularly good ones as they both involve sports that have been the traditional bastions of those blowing the anti-doping trumpet

Few Athletes Admit to Performance-Enhancing Drug Use

A survey of 375 elite international athletes found that while few admitted to either knowingly or unknowingly taking performance-enhancing drugs, many claim to know other athletes who take illegal substances.

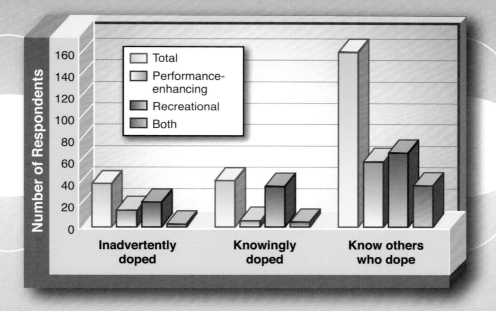

Taken from: Aidan Moran, Suzanne Guerin, and Kate Kirby, "The Development and Validation of a Doping Attitudes and Behavior Scale," May 16, 2008. www.wada-ama.org/rtecontent/document/Moran_Final_Report.pdf.

the loudest. Yes, comes the immediate response, but when you take performance enhancers, *you* are not competing. It is some super-you; you are performing way beyond your natural capacity. People who use this line of argument are simply (and conveniently) omitting the impact of new technology. Don't running spikes, Windsuits and composite hockey sticks do exactly the same thing? Anyone arguing from an "all athletes need equal footing" perspective is going to have to go the whole way and have us all passing the baton barefoot and naked. Furthermore, such veiled references to the sacred natural boundaries or sacrosanct impermeability of the body seem a blatant endorsement of another double standard, considering the blind eye turned towards other types of invasive enhancements like Botox, Ritalin and Viagra.

This then is the double standard present today in professional sport: we allow technological improvements in equipment to help our athletes, but declare using (some) technological improvements in synthetic stimulants for the same ends illegal. Today's athletes have such sport-specific, regimented training regimes, not to mention all the added bonuses afforded by improved equipment, that performance enhancers simply represent the next logical step in trying to realize maximum human potential. The fact that I break the world record for the 100 metre sprint while using a performance enhancer doesn't detract from the fact that it was me who broke the record—it doesn't make it any less an essentially human achievement. Not just anyone taking the performance enhancer would break that record; I still need all my usual training and commitment. In short, I still need to be the best. It merely means that with the help of performance enhancers, I can be even better.

A Separate Issue

This is not an argument for all types of steroids to be made available whole-sale to the public; I feel that this could well endanger many lives. Some athletes might well want to argue that they don't want to risk their lives to compete and win, and that others' willingness to do this puts them at a disadvantage. The "harms" argument is, however, a separate issue, and has little effect on claims concerning unfair advantages. Moreover the fact is that many safe performance enhancers are banned alongside those that are dangerous—why not just ban the dangerous ones? I am not offering a complete policy on performance enhancers; I am merely asking us to rethink our intuitive reactions towards them, as arguing that "inside the body" technology gives athletes an unfair edge runs into the problems discussed above.

SIX

Performance-Enhancing Drugs Should Be Allowed in Sports

Jesse Haggard

In the following viewpoint Jesse Haggard agrees that steroids do give an advantage to athletes who use them. However, he asserts, steroids will not automatically transform the user into a better athlete or improve his or her skills. Haggard maintains that the concern over steroid use in sports has spilled over into steroid use in health care, but the two areas should remain completely separate. In Haggard's opinion, steroids should be allowed in sports in order to assure that steroid use in health care remains available and legal. Haggard, the former medical director of a naturopathic medical clinic in Phoenix that dispensed steroids, had his license to practice medicine revoked because of irregularities in his record keeping.

There would be no debate about the use of steroids, unless steroid use produced a significant effect on people. My research and firsthand experience treating more than two thousand patients has, without a doubt, demonstrated steroid use causes a great effect in most people. In fact, anabolic steroid medication was the single most effective medication I prescribed that would cause patients to notice a significant difference in their health. This declared effect is without specifying a positive or negative difference, but a general effect for both men and women. To further demonstrate the point, most people know about steroids' ability to help promote muscle strength and mass in athletes; however, anabolic steroids even increase muscle strength and mass without exercise in an average person. The muscle building and strength effect is more pronounced with exercise, but it just demonstrates the effective potential of anabolic steroids. . . .

Do Steroids Provide Athletes an Unfair Advantage?

Absolutely! In my experience, there is an unmistakable advantage to the user of anabolic steroids in regard to physical performance in sports. The positive effects . . . produce increased performance of physical capabilities, with even a superhuman potential, and faster healing in most people. On the other hand, taking steroids will not automatically make someone a better athlete. Most sports require balance, hand-eye coordination and good judgment that can only be achieved from repeatedly playing or performing the activity required for the sport. Steroids simply allow the person's body to play with more strength, stamina and less downtime, but steroids will not increase athletic skills. The stamina component also requires concomitant [concurrent] exercise from the user to achieve an increase in endurance. Thus, steroid use improves athletic potential that may be unfair to other nonusing athletes, but effort and skill are still required from the athlete to advance to a professional athletic level.

Sports Interfering with Healthcare

The concern of steroid use in sports has become so extreme that efforts to restrict steroid use in sports have spilled over to healthcare. Since the recent steroid problems in professional baseball were highlighted by the media, the healthcare field has suffered unwarranted scrutiny and negative changes. Medications have been limited and discontinued altogether from government influence. Compounding pharmacies have been greatly restricted on their ability to generate custom medications for patients, as well. Patients' private and personal healthcare information has been inappropriately exposed to the government and public. Many doctors and pharmacies have been criminally penalized for their involvement in steroid medications used for medical purposes.

These changes in healthcare are completely uncalled for, and steroid use in sports may simply be a shroud and excuse for the government or other organizations to gain more power and economic advantage. The government has increased restrictions and control in healthcare, and many large drug companies have increased revenues all in the name of sport fairness and equality. I encourage the public to beware of such drastic changes made so quickly and hope the public opposes these changes to preserve their freedoms in healthcare.

Fairness, Equality and Antidoping

The current "no tolerance" steroid policy in Olympic and professional sports is not creating fairness and equality among athletes. Prohibiting steroid use in competitive sports is an interesting idea to promote fairness and equality, but the inability to accurately test and enforce policies against steroid use makes such policies unrealistic. Testing athletes for steroid use who are in Olympic and professional sports does not cease all steroid use in sports. Testing for steroids only reduces steroid use. Athletes can usually continue to use steroids, regardless of the steroid screening test used. The athletes may need to reduce their dosage, change steroid products or add other medications to pass a steroid test, but *none* of the antidoping tests employed today detect steroid use 100%. There are methods to falsely pass every antidoping test used today. More sensitive tests are possible, but due to lack of demand, commercial development or financial limitations, these more accurate tests are not used.

Technology has never been evenly distributed among the world and neither has the opportunity for using performance enhancers. Testing athletes for performance-enhancing substances will always be a "cat-and-mouse" game. Tests for detecting

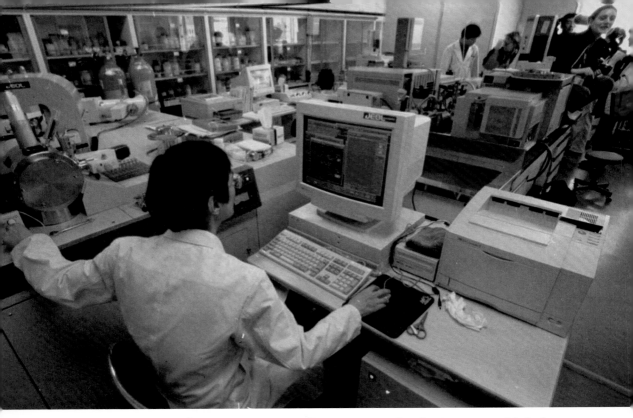

A technician processes drug tests at the doping control lab for the Olympic Games. Currently no antidoping test can detect steroid use 100 percent of the time.

performance enhancers will always be developed after the performance enhancer, and the delay creates opportunity for doping athletes to have an advantage over all other athletes. History has proven these points many times over. For example, the Olympic Games have had numerous medal recalls from athletes due to doping over the last 30 years. Some athletes used substances that the World Anti-Doping Agency [WADA] was unaware of or did not test for, demonstrating technology inequality. A case in point was the use of steroids in German Olympic athletes. The support of their country gave the German athletes an opportunity to use performance enhancers that the other athletes did not have. Creating inequality may not always be purposeful. With the constant development of new substances and techniques to enhance performance, many athletes, coaches and trainers do not initially understand what substances or techniques may create unacceptable user advantage and playing field inequality. The same relationship exists for methods to falsely pass antidoping tests. Methods to falsely pass an anti-doping test will be developed before provisions of the tests to counter these methods may be developed. Once again many Olympic athletes, although identified by some other means later, found methods to falsely pass all of the antidoping tests required for athletic participation. Despite the good intentions, the antidoping agencies commonly identified doping athletes after the sporting event is over and the other contestants have already lost their competitive opportunity forever. Therefore, inequalities in technology create unfair opportunities for athletes to use performance enhancers.

Fairness, Equality, and Other Performance Enhancers

The next item to address is steroids are not unique for their ability to enhance athletic performance. The purpose of anti-doping programs is "To protect the Athletes' fundamental right to participate in a doping-free sport and thus promote health, fairness and equality for athletes worldwide . . ." (WADA 2003). Yet, there are many substances capable of enhancing athletic performance that are widely available, and most are legal to use in any sport or are unable to test for. What makes steroids so different in sports? Creatine is a great example to compare to steroids because most people are familiar with creatine. Creatine has been shown to increase all of the same physical performance parameters that steroids enhance including, but not limited to, maximum lifting strength, vertical jump performance, enhanced sprint performance, high-intensity exercise performance, maximal exercise capacity and gains in fat-free mass. All of these performance-enhancing effects from creatine seem to be contradictory to creating "fairness and equality for athletes," yet creatine use is allowed in all sports, and the International Olympic Committee (IOC) supports its use among athletes. If the real issue is creating fairness and equality for athletes, then I do not see the difference between creatine and steroids in regard to competitive sports. Both are naturally occurring chemical substances in the human body, and their concentrations may be increased with diet changes, such as eating more meat. Each substance may be purified to achieve supraphysiological levels in the human body and corresponds with increased performance and superhuman function. Both creatine and steroid use have been associated with many records achieved in sports. Creatine use may have negative health consequences (few safety studies have been performed at creatine doses above 20 grams per day) and works in a dose-dependent fashion like steroids. So once again, what makes steroid use in sports such a unique topic?

What Do We Do with This Data?

So far, I have proposed several main concepts:

- Steroids have a great effect on most people, and the effects of steroids can be both positive and negative.
- Steroid deficiencies are prevalent in the general population and, although more common in the elderly, may occur at any adult age.
- The effects of steroids are dose-dependent, and the user may achieve superhuman function.
- Steroids can create an unfair advantage for athletes.
- Testing for steroids to detect doping athletes or athletes who use steroids for performance enhancement is not 100% accurate.
- Steroids are only one of many physical performance-enhancing substances known and widely available today.
- The "no tolerance" antidoping laws have not created fairness and equality for athletes in the past and nor do they now.

As a physician, I am weakly concerned with the possible influence steroids may have on sports, and I am amazed that professional sports can significantly impact the possible tools I have available. The choice of tools physicians have available can easily equate to life or death and a significant difference in someone's quality of life. My priorities are people's health instead of sports. Nevertheless, it is not my sole decision. Thus, as a society, we need to decide if professional sports should dictate medicine in our country. I present extreme examples of each decision to demonstrate the range of possibilities and their potential effects.

No Steroids and Sports

If we choose as a country to let professional sports be a priority before healthcare, we could give up steroid use in medicine altogether and end the debate. The benefits of this decision would be less availability for professional athletes to use steroids to achieve an unfair advantage over other sports participants, and no adverse effects would be experienced in the general population. Screening professional athletes for illegal steroid use would be easier, because there would be a "no tolerance" policy. If any steroid is detected, the person is disqualified to participate in professional sports. The downside of the decision to forbid the use of steroids in medicine would reduce quality of life in many people, most likely increase death in a significant portion of the public, cause a powerful tool to be lost for physicians and a guarantee to increase the black market use of steroids by our general population. I boldly claim that people would use black market sources if steroids were made illegal, because it has occurred previously. In my experience, when patients were unable to obtain steroids through a legitimate physician or pharmacy, many purchased steroids on the black market. History usually repeats itself, and I expect most people would buy from the black market again if steroids became illegal. A significant portion of the public currently uses steroids, and I doubt they would give up their use so quickly after they have experienced beneficial results. Overall, the action of this decision is extreme and a poor choice for the well-being of the general population.

Allowing Steroids in Sports

An opposite choice is we recognize that steroids have a great potential for our population, and part of our population are athletes who could experience the same benefits. Many people who enjoy being athletes may have medical conditions that prevent them from participating in professional sports. An extreme example is a male athlete who incurred severe testicular trauma and requires steroid treatment for physiological steroid replacement. If people like this can receive treatments and overcome their medical condition to the extent of achieving a professional level of performance, I feel they should have the opportunity to play regardless of the treatment or condition. These people did not choose their medical conditions, so why should they be denied good health and the chance to be involved in professional sports? . . . Furthermore, allowing steroid use in sports may uncover a great source of older athletes who want to extend

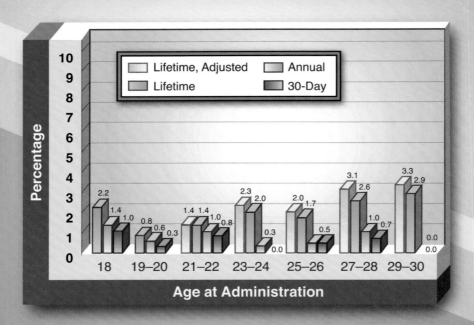

Steroid Use Increases with Age

Note: Lifetime prevalence estimates were adjusted for inconsistency in self-reports of drug use over time.

Taken from: Monitoring the Future National Survey Results on Drug Use, 1975–2007, Volume II: College Students and Adults Ages 19–45, 2008. www.monitoringthefuture.org/pus/monographs/vol2_2007.pdf.

their existing athletic career or begin a new athletic path. I often hear from middle-aged people that they chose a career path or educational path instead of participating in sports when they were younger and that they have now missed their opportunity to be involved in sports, especially at a professional level. What if these people created another opportunity for themselves to engage in professional sports by restoring their bodies to a more youthful state? It could potentially reduce the age limitation we currently know in sports today. In addition, I believe allowing steroids in sports will create more of a fair playing field. There are a number of athletes that have learned tricks to pass steroid testing and use steroids in their sport. Being able to use steroids in your sport against others who can't because they do not know how or just chose to follow the rules is not fair to me. Allowing all athletes the ability to use steroids is the only way the sports world will ever be 100% fair. If athletes who do not need steroid replacement use steroids solely for athletic performance, they can suffer the adverse effects that accompany the superhuman functions. I think people should be responsible for themselves. Athletes who do not use steroids unnecessarily will most likely have longer careers than those who use them inappropriately, because they will not have the adverse health effects to hinder their performance.

The Separate Topic of Steroids in Sports

Whatever choice is made with steroids and sports, it should be separate from steroids in medicine. In my opinion, the positive effects I have observed with steroid use far outweigh any negative impact steroids might be having in sports. I have observed firsthand dramatic changes in patients' quality of life with steroid use, both in females and males. Since adverse effects may occur with steroid use, I believe physician monitoring seems necessary to protect the public from these adverse effects. Careful attention is required to create a workable solution for everyone, but medicine and sports should be two separate and independent topics. . . .

Demystifying Steroids

Medical experts and the media have done a great job at driving fear into the public in regard to the dangers of steroid use. However, through an open mind and clinical experience involving thousands of people, steroids have been demystified for me and my patients. Steroids are a great tool in medicine and have the potential to be demystified for you, as well. Most of the dangers of steroids may be avoided with educated use. Proper use of steroids may offer significant quality of life improvements to both individuals and society as a whole. I want to have steroids available to me if there comes a day that they may improve my quality of life. Furthermore, additional research involving steroids my help us advance our understanding of the human body and possibly unlock our true human potential.

I believe steroid use in sports should be an independent topic from steroid use in medicine. Furthermore, restricting steroid use in medicine and availability to the general public may or may not affect steroid use in sports.

The current "no tolerance" policy is not effective for creating fair competition among athletes. Prohibiting steroid use in sports is a good idea to promote fairness among athletes, but the inability to test and enforce it makes it unrealistic. The "no tolerance" policy is being inadequately managed because there are methods to falsely pass every test currently used for detecting illegal steroid use. Athletic performance is enhanced by steroid use, but many other chemical substances enhance athletic performance, as well. Steroid use in athletes is not different than many other chemical substances that enhance athletic performance that are widely available, not illegal, not popularly known or unable to be tested for. There are many medical conditions that may be treated with steroids. Persons with medical conditions requiring steroid treatment should not be denied access to participate in professional sports just because they have a particular medical condition. Only allowing steroids for people with steroid deficiencies would be complicated to manage because creating acceptable ranges or parameters is problematic in regard to steroid use in athletes. Therefore, I feel the overall best solution to our current sports situation is to allow steroid use and all other performance-enhancing substances in sports.

SEVEN

Performance-Enhancing Drugs Do Not Belong in Sports

Sal Marinello

Sal Marinello, a personal trainer, assistant high school football coach, and weight-lifting coach, asserts that the arguments supporting performance-enhancing drugs in sports are illogical and blur the issue of right and wrong. He contends that the majority of athletes want to compete drug-free. Marinello maintains that if the use of steroids and other drugs are permitted in sporting competitions, then all athletes will have to use performance-enhancing drugs in order to remain competitive. Performance-enhancing drugs are and should remain illegal, he asserts, and athletes caught using performance-enhancing drugs should have their achievements for the entire season erased.

I rarely call people out. Really. But a . . . column by a writer named Patrick Hruby posted on ESPN.com's Page 2, titled "Let The Juicing Begin", leaves me little choice. This guy has no clue as to what he's talking about when it comes to performance-enhancing drugs and whether or not Barry Bonds is right to use them, regardless of who he writes for or what experts in the field that he has gathered quotes from.

Sal Marinello, "Don't Fall Prey to the Steroids-Are-Okay Argument," http://blogcritics.org, March 23, 2006. Reproduced by permission of the author: www.SalMarinello.com; Publisher: www.PersonalTrainerCoach.com; Publisher: www.HealthAndFitnessAdvice.com; Contributor, Blogcritics.org; http://blogcritics.org/writers/sal-marinello.

An Intellectually Lazy Approach

In this disjointed piece the author starts off by quoting, and then agreeing with, Olympic bust Bode Miller's position that sports doping should be permitted. Bode's critical reasoning skills allowed him to come up with this position on the subject.

According to Miller, "I don't think it's (using performance-enhancing drugs) a really big deal, I think people should be able to do what they want to do." Mr. Hruby then questions whether Miller can be considered a credible source for any kind of information, and somehow reaches the following conclusion:

> The messenger seems like a dope. But the message? The more I think about it, the more I'm convinced it has merit. Really, why not let athletes juice?

Things spiral downhill from here as Hruby follows the usual intellectually lazy and dishonest path used by those who take the approach of *"Really, why not let athletes juice?"*

Hruby starts out with the old stand-by that despite the money spent on testing, for every step the authorities take to close a loophole, another loophole is created. He even quotes renowned steroid expert Dr. Charles Yesalis who says that testing only catches the dumb and the lazy.

If local police departments took this same approach to law enforcement our country would be in real trouble. Rudy Giuliani cleaned up New York City in large part because A) most criminals ARE dumb and/or lazy and B) Rudy supported the police department in their efforts to stop the most petty of petty criminal activities that were perpetrated by the dumbest and laziest criminals. As a result the *overall* crime rate in New York City dropped to an all-time low, including the rate of the most serious crimes like murder.

Another huge problem with the philosophy that testing only catches the dumb—especially when talking about Bonds and friends—is that Major League Baseball [MLB] has had a laughable testing policy. If MLB had any real policy they would have caught the guys using steroids and the other drugs.

The author uses the Barry Bonds steroid controversy to point out Major League Baseball's "laughable" drug testing policy that he says catches only the stupid or lazy offender.

Is Competition Really Relative?

From here, Hruby hits us with the next justification of steroid users, the one that says "Competitive Integrity Is Relative" or "CIIR." The prime example of the relativity of competition that's used by those who promote this nonsense, is that Babe Ruth hit his home runs in an era where there were no black ballplayers in the major leagues. The logic employed by the CIIR follows the line that since there were no blacks in the league in the day of the Babe, his numbers are the result of an unlevel playing field and should be considered in this light.

This position assumes that the players in the major leagues during Ruth's era were not as good as those toiling in the Negro

The U.S. Anti-Doping Agency (USADA) tests amateur athletes in Olympic, Paralympic, and Pan American sports. Out-of-competition testing is done without any advance notice and can be done at the athlete's home or training facility; in-competition tests are done at the sporting event. In 2008 USADA tested 7,690 American athletes and found 25 violations of its antidoping rules.

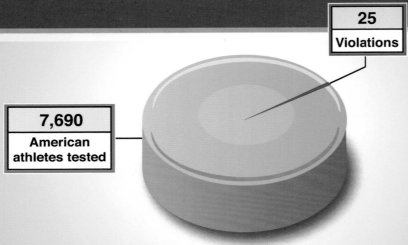

25 Violations

7,690 American athletes tested

Taken from: U.S. Anti-Doping Agency, "U.S. Anti-Doping Agency Announces Final Testing Numbers for 2008," February 20, 2009.

Leagues, which is a position of dubious merit. There is no way to prove this point, just like there is no way to accurately compare players from different eras.

If you're in the CIIR camp, statistics cannot be used as evidence of the superiority of the Negro League players because they did not play against any *white* ballplayers. The only way Negro League stats can be used to "prove" that black players were as good or superior to white players, is if you believe—across the board—that black players are inherently better than white players. This is just as wrong as believing that white players are inherently better than black players.

Apples and Oranges

Back to the present. . . . Hruby and his ilk want you to believe that individual players who have made the decision to use steroids—and cheat—are somehow justified in their actions because there has never been a level playing field in sports. Equating steroid use with the segregation of baseball is comparing apples and oranges.

Believers in CIIR are treading in dangerous water and should be careful. If you believe in CIIR—in order to be consistent and credible—you have to believe that this relativity of competition occurs in every era and not just the era of the Babe. And not in just baseball.

Proponets of CIIR use the segregation of baseball when looking at Ruth's numbers, but they don't do the same thing when looking at Henry Aaron's numbers. Hank Aaron started his career before the league was totally integrated, and played the majority of his career when Latin Americans were in short supply as well. If you agree with CIIR you have to look at Aaron's numbers with this same level of skepticism as you look at Ruth's, as Aaron played in an era where both blacks and Latin Americans were under-represented.

And now that Asians are considered to be as good as any other group of people who play baseball, can Bonds' numbers—or the numbers of any of today's players—be looked at from the CIIR standpoint since there aren't a lot of Asians in MLB? And thanks to "Down With Fidel" Castro, Cubans are still underrepresented. Does this further diminish the accomplishments of present day MLB players?

A Neverending Path of "What Ifs"

The problem with this line of thought is that it is just plain silly and it sends you down a neverending path of "what ifs" and "what abouts." The author himself brings up the issue of "plate crowders" and guys—like Bonds—who use big protective elbow protectors as as example of the benefits the current generation enjoys that the old-timers would never have gotten away with.

And what about artificial turf? How many routine ground balls have been turned into base hits because of turf? What about the better travel conditions today's players enjoy? How about the advances in medical treatment and conditioning? What about the fact that today's ballplayers are so well paid that all they have to worry about is playing ball, when in the old days ball players had to a find jobs in the off season? What about, what about, what about? And then there are all the other sports that you'd have to reevaluate using the canard [false story] of CIIR.

Hruby goes on to point out that Lasik [eye] and Tommy John [elbow] surgeries are procedures that can help a player perform better; and this is true. But these procedures deal with allowing a player to regain something that they have lost due to injury and/or aging, and don't allow a person to do something that they weren't capable of beforehand. Neither of these procedures are illegal, either. Furthermore, I don't recall any pitchers undergoing elective Tommy John surgery so that they could add a few extra miles per hour to their fast ball. Do you think there are any legit surgeons out there who would perform this procedure if it wasn't necessary?

Blurring the Lines

Here's a statement that illustrates Hruby's staggering lack of understanding of this issue. He claims that steroids ". . . actually allow athletes to work harder and more effectively, much like a good strength coach."

This kind of equivocation blurs all lines of right versus wrong, legal versus illegal, minor issue versus major issue; kind of like equating a parking ticket with grand theft auto. It's like saying, *"Both of these issues involve automobiles and breaking the rules, so hey, what's the difference?"*

Nowhere in Hruby's article does he talk about the athletes who *don't* want to stick themselves with needles and play guinea pig in order to compete. Hruby gives no thought to the guys and gals who *don't* want to use substances that may or may not result in medical problems down the line, nor does he discuss the fact that the vast majority of athletes want to compete while clean. Hruby doesn't mention the athletes who have been over-shadowed by the cheaters, or mention the money, awards and accolades that have been stolen from the clean athletes by the dirty athletes.

Think about how you would feel if you had to take a drug, or do something that you are opposed to doing, in order to compete for your job.

He doesn't mention that Bonds—with all of his modern conveniences—is literally limping to break a record that a clean Aaron sprinted through.

Inconvenient Realities

Despite what Hruby would have you think, most athletes *don't* want to resort to taking these drugs, a fact that Hruby convenient-ly leaves out of his article. These realities are too inconvenient for people like Hruby to deal with. They choose to take the easy way out, throw up their hands and quit. If you apply this approach to other issues in our society—vexing and otherwise—we'd have chaos and anarchy.

Take a Stand

How about taking a stand on an issue? Have the courage to say that cheaters will always try to cheat, but we are always going to try to catch them, and when we catch them we will punish them severely.

How about a season ban combined with wiping out any achievements of players caught cheating, steroids, corked bat or otherwise? There is no acknowlegement of [Canadian sprinter] Ben Johnson's drug-aided record so why not do the same in pro sports?

And if the players don't feel that they are cheating by using these drugs, why don't *they* come out and tell us so? Why is it always "the other guy" that supports the unfettered use of performance-enhancing drugs and not the athletes themselves?

An Insulting Argument

Finally, Hruby insults us all when he says that we are all hypocrites:

> We pop recreational Viagra. We study for exams by popping Ritalin. We shed extra pounds with gastric bypass surgery, a grisly medical procedure rife with ghastly side effects (gallstones, anemia, pulmonary embolism). We enhance ourselves on a daily basis—for performance, for fun, for petty vanity. Because, quite frankly, we can.

This tells us more about the author than it does about "us." Because people as individuals choose to do any of these things is not a reason to paint—and damn—all of "us" with the same broad brush. It's not a reason that people should be allowed to cheat during competition. How Viagra, misusing Ritalin and gastric bypass surgery relates to cheating in sports is a mystery.

Rather than enlighten people, articles like this just serve to further muddy the waters with misinformation, half truths and faulty logic.

EIGHT

Using Steroids in Baseball Is Beneficial to the Game

Jose Canseco

> Jose Canseco hit 462 home runs during his seventeen-year career as a professional baseball player. In the following viewpoint, taken from his book *Juiced: Wild Times, Rampant 'Roids, Smash Hits, and How Baseball Got Big,* he argues that steroids make players better athletes, and better athletes make the games more exciting. Canseco maintains that spectators want to see exciting games and be entertained by superstar athletes. Therefore, he asserts, athletes, sporting organizations, ball club owners, and fans all benefit when athletes use steroids.

These past few years, all you had to do was turn on a radio or flip to a sports cable channel, and you could count on hearing some blowhard give you his opinion about steroids and baseball and what it says about our society and blah blah blah. Well, enough already. I'm tired of hearing such short-sighted crap from people who have no idea what they're talking about. Steroids are here to stay. That's a fact. I guarantee it. Steroids are the future. By the time my eight-year-old daughter, Josie, has graduated from high school, a majority of all professional athletes—in all sports—will be taking steroids. And believe it or not, that's good news.

Steroids Are Serious

Let's be clear what we are talking about. In no way, shape, or form, do I endorse the use of steroids without proper medical advice and thorough expert supervision. I'll say it again: Steroids are serious. They are nothing to mess around with casually, and if anything, devoting yourself to the systematic use of steroids means you have to stay away from recreational drugs. I was never into that stuff anyway, cocaine and all that, but if you're going to work with steroids, you have to get used to clean living, smart eating, and taking care of yourself by getting plenty of rest and not overtaxing your body.

I'm especially critical of anyone who starts playing around with steroids too early, when they are barely old enough to shave and not even fully grown yet. Your body is already raging with hormones at that age, and the last thing you want to do is wreak havoc with your body's natural balance. If you want to turn yourself into a nearly superhuman athlete, the way I did, you need to wait until you have matured into adulthood. That way your body can handle it. And you shouldn't fool yourself into thinking that all you need to do is just read a few articles on steroids, either. What you need to do is to absorb every scrap of information and insight on the subject—to become an expert on the subject, the way I did.

We're talking about the future here. I have no doubt whatsoever that intelligent, informed use of steroids, combined with human growth hormone, will one day be so accepted that everybody will be doing it. Steroid use will be more common than Botox is now. Every baseball player and pro athlete will be using at least low levels of steroids. As a result, baseball and other sports will be more exciting and entertaining. Human life will be improved, too. We will live longer and better. And maybe we'll love longer and better, too.

We will be able to look good and have strong, fit bodies well into our sixties and beyond. It's called evolution, and there is no stopping it. All these people crying about steroids in baseball now will look as foolish in a few years as the people who said John F. Kennedy was crazy to say the United States would put a man on the moon. People who see the future earlier than others are always feared and misunderstood.

The public needs to be informed about the reality of steroids and how they have affected the lives of many star baseball players, including me. Have I used steroids? You bet I did. Did steroids make me a better baseball player? Of course they did. If I had it all

Viewpoint author and professional baseball player Jose Canseco discusses his use of steroids in his book Juiced. He believes that steroid use in sports should be legal.

to do over again, would I live a steroid-enriched life? Yes, I would. Do I have any regrets or qualms about relying on chemicals to help me hit a baseball so far? To be honest, no, I don't.

We human beings are made up of chemicals. High school chemistry students learn to recite "CHOPKINS CaFe," which is all the chemical elements that make up the human body: carbon, hydrogen, oxygen, phosphorous, potassium, iodine, nitrogen, sulfur, calcium, and iron. Maybe it bothers some people to think of our bodies as just a collection of those elements, but I find it comforting.

Steroids Can Be Used Safely

I like studying the body and how it works. I like knowing all about what makes us stronger and faster. If you learn about the chemicals that make up life, and study the hormones coursing through our bloodstreams that give our bodies instructions, you can learn how to improve your health through controlled use of steroids. And you can do it safely.

Yes, you heard me right: Steroids, used correctly, will not only make you stronger and sexier, they will also make you healthier. Certain steroids, used in proper combinations, can cure certain diseases. Steroids will give you a better quality of life and also drastically slow down the aging process.

If people learn how to use steroids and growth hormone properly, especially as they get older—sixty, seventy, eighty years old—their way of living will change completely. If you start young enough, when you are in your twenties, thirties, and forties, and use steroids properly, you can probably slow the aging process by fifteen or twenty years. I'm forty years old, but I look much younger—and I can still do everything the way I could when I was twenty-five.

When I talk in detail about steroids and how I single-handedly changed the game of baseball by introducing them into the game, I am saying what everyone in baseball has known for years. To all my critics, to everyone who wants to turn this into a debate about me, Jose Canseco, let me quote my favorite actor (besides Arnold Schwarzenegger, that is) and say: You can't *handle* the truth.

Steroids Make the Game Exciting

That is the story of baseball in recent years. Everyone in the game has been hoping the lie could last as long as possible. They wanted steroids in the game to make it more exciting, hoping they would be able to build its popularity back up after the disastrous cancellation of the 1994 World Series. So when I taught other players how to use steroids, no one lifted a finger to stop me. When I educated trainers and others on how to inject players with steroids, there was nothing standing in my way. Directly or indirectly, nearly everyone in baseball was complicit.

How do I know that? I was known as the godfather of steroids in baseball. I introduced steroids into the big leagues back in 1985, and taught other players how to use steroids and growth hormone. Back then, weight lifting was taboo in baseball. The teams didn't have weight-lifting programs. Teams didn't allow it. But once they saw what I could do as a result of my weight lifting, they said, "My God, if it's working for Jose, it's gotta work for a lot of players."

So all of a sudden ballparks were being built with brand-new, high-tech weight-lifting facilities, and at the older ballparks they were moving stuff around and remodeling to make room for weight rooms. I definitely restructured the way the game was played. Because of my influence, and my example, there were dramatic changes in the way that players looked and the way they played. That was because of changes in their nutrition, their approach to fitness and weight lifting, and their steroid intake and education.

If you asked any player who was the one who knew about steroids, they'd all tell you: Jose Canseco.

Who do you go to when you want information on steroids?

Jose Canseco.

Who do you go to if you wanted to know if you were using it properly?

Jose Canseco. . . .

Some of baseball's superstars—some of whom are reported to have taken performance-enhancing drugs during their careers—recorded suspiciously high increases in their statistics in just a year.

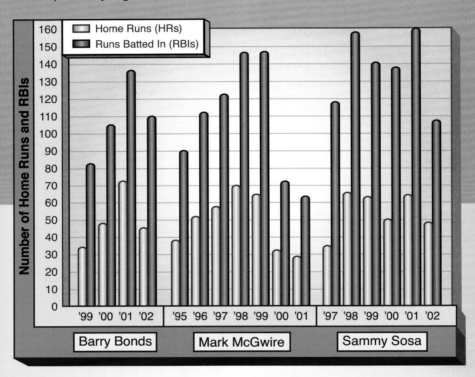

Taken from: Jose Canseco, *Vindicated: Big Names, Big Liars, and the Battle to Save Baseball,* Simon Spotlight, a division of Simon & Schuster, 2008.

A Steroid Guru

Back when I first started using steroids, I tracked down as many books as I could find on the subject, and I studied the science behind steroids. I started becoming something like a guru. I wanted to know everything about each steroid and what it did, especially pertaining to athletes and sports and baseball. Could it make me faster? Could it make me stronger? Could it make me injury-free? I started experimenting on myself, using my own body to see what steroid could do what. Today, I probably know more about steroids and what steroids can do for the human body than any layman in the world.

I believe every steroid out there can be used safely and beneficially—it's all a question of dosage. Some steroids you cycle off and on, depending on the dose. You just have to make sure you give your liver enough time to filter them out. There are other steroids that have very low toxicity levels. Those can be taken continuously by most healthy people. It just depends. Growth hormone? You can use that all year round. Same thing with your Equipoise, your Winstrols, your Decas—taken properly, those are fine all year round. But something like Anadrol, and some high dosages of testosterone—those have to be moderated, taken more selectively. This is all important because when ballplayers talk about steroids, they really mean a combination of steroids and growth hormone, and that requires some serious planning if you don't want to get yourself in trouble. . . .

Everyone Has Used Steroids

Have other superstars used steroids? If you don't know the answer, you've been skimming, not reading. The challenge is not to find a top player who has used steroids. The challenge is to find a top player who *hasn't*. No one who reads [my] book from cover to cover will have any doubt that steroids are a huge part of baseball, and always will be, no matter what crazy toothless testing schemes the powers that be might dream up.

Is it cheating to do what everyone wants you to do? Are players the only ones to blame for steroids when Donald Fehr and the other bosses of the Major League Players' Association fought for years to make sure players wouldn't be tested for steroids? Is it all that secret when the owners of the game put out the word that they want home runs and excitement, making sure that everyone from trainers to managers to clubhouse attendants understands that whatever it is the players are doing to become superhuman, they sure ought to keep it up?

People want to be entertained at the ballpark. They want baseball to be fun and exciting. Home runs are fun and exciting. They are easy for even the most casual fan to appreciate. Steroid-enhanced athletes hit more home runs. So yes, I have personally reshaped the game of baseball through my example and my teaching. More than that, I am glad that soon enough the work I've done will help reshape the way millions of you out there live your lives, too. Why should only top athletes with huge salaries reap the benefits of the revolution in biotechnology that will define our times? Why shouldn't everyone get to ride the wave?

NINE

Using Steroids in Baseball Is Not Beneficial to the Game

Armstrong Williams

> Armstrong Williams is a contributor to *Human Events* and has been called "one of the most recognized conservative voices in America" by *The Washington Post*. In the following viewpoint Williams argues that the release of the Mitchell Report on steroid use in professional baseball proved that many of the best athletes in the sport were cheaters. The players, owners, and Major League Baseball itself were all to blame for the steroid era, which could have been prevented by simply working out a solution when performance-enhancing drugs first showed signs of impacting the sports world. Williams adds that the increase in runs scored per game during the steroid era could have been achieved without the players using performance-enhancing drugs, citing reasons such as smaller ballparks, the tighter-wound ball, and the expansion of the league to prove that steroids were not the reason behind the explosion of home runs. Yet every home run hit in the steroid era, Williams argues, could have been the result of cheating through the use of performance-enhancing drugs.

Like millions of other baseball fans around the world, I had mixed emotions when the Mitchell Report went public. . . . On one hand, I was glad that Major League Baseball finally and

Former senator George Mitchell, author of the Mitchell Report, swears in to testify before the U.S. House of Representatives Committee on Oversight and Government Reform about his investigation into illegal steroid use by players in Major League Baseball.

formally admitted that steroids, human growth hormone, and performance enhancing drugs have plagued the sports industry. However, I was disappointed to see that some of my favorite athletes are cheaters. Although I suspected (as did many fans) that it was somehow unnatural for big leaguers like Barry Bonds and Sammy Sosa to become bigger and physically stronger at the end of their careers, it would be un-American of me to blame them without sufficient proof. Now, with the release of the Mitchell Report, the problem has finally come to light, allowing Commissioner Bud Selig's, players, owners, and agents to take real action towards cleaning up the mess.

Baseball, the National Pastime, has entertained Americans since the 1800's, and, for perhaps just as long, been the center of controversy. From the Black Sox scandal in 1919, in which eight players were accused of throwing the World Series, to the Pete Rose betting scandal, to the Pittsburg Drug Trials in 1985, to the steroid era, Baseball and controversy have gone together for over 100 years. The debate shouldn't be whether bad things happen in the game—because we know they have and will continue to happen—the debate should be how we handle the problem.

Who Was to Blame?

Major League Baseball and the players Association botched the steroid era from the beginning. Years ago, when the first inkling of performance enhancing drugs hit the world of sports, the owners and players could have and should have worked out a blameless truce that would serve all interested parties and eliminated that form of cheating going forward.

A clean game, on the surface, may not seem to serve team owners who clearly benefit at the ticket office from higher scoring games with lots of homeruns. However, as we've learned from the Mitchell Report, there were numerous pitchers (including potential Hall of Famer Roger Clemens) who were also using these illegal enhancers. So, although teams during the steroid era were producing more runs per game than ever, the higher run production cannot be attributed to stronger hitters alone. Factors like the tighter wound ball, smaller ballparks, the expansion of the league, uniformed strike zones, and state of the art weight training all contributed to the rise in runs per game. Thus, though many owners, [say] for example Peter McGowan of the San Francisco Giants, reaped the rewards of their juiced hitters scoring more runs, the fact remains that the increased attendance during the steroid era could have occurred without the players breaking the law.

Owners should have seen that their investments—their players—were hurting themselves both literally (performance-enhancing drugs have been shown to cause long term physical

Baseball Fans Think Steroid Users Should Be Punished

In a survey of fans of professional baseball, most said that the players named in the Mitchell Report about steroid abuse in Major League Baseball should be punished.

Shortly before George Mitchell submitted his report on steroid use in baseball to Commissioner Bud Selig, fans were asked: Do you think Bud Selig should—or should not—punish current Major League Baseball players who are named in the report for having used steroids in the past?

	November 30–December 2, 2007 Percentage
Yes, should punish those players	60
• Suspend those players	43
• Fine but not suspend those players	16
• Unsure	1
No, should not punish those players	37
No opinion	3

Combined responses based on professional baseball fans.

Taken from: *USA Today*/Gallup Poll, November 30–December 2, 2007.

and emotional damage) and figuratively (nobody likes a cheater), and forced the player's union to accept some sort of drug testing, monitoring, and educational program.

More so than the owners, the players themselves bungled the steroid issue. The players who used were cheaters. And the players who didn't were enablers. The players could have gone to their union representatives and argued that all suffer when a few use drugs. When a few bad apples appear, the whole tree looks bad. Those honorable players who avoided performance enhancers should have united and demanded that the playing field be leveled by comprehensive drug testing.

Moving Forward

So here we are, ten years or so into this mess, and still no real resolution. The damning Mitchell Report named names, and the whole world now doubts just about every run that was scored since the Bash Brothers (noted users Mark McGwire and Jose Canseco of the Oakland Athletics) came onto the national scene in the late 1980's. The answer to the problem is simple: learn from the past to make the future better.

We cannot fix our past mistakes, but we can certainly use them to better ourselves. Major League Baseball must do the same. They must hire an independent outside organization to develop and enforce the strictest drug policy in sports. Year-around random testing is only the beginning. New technology, better research, improved education, transparent testing, harsh consequences, and mandatory meetings with everyone involved will make the program more reliable and valid. Just like they recovered from the Black Sox scandal or the strike of 1994, baseball will recover from the steroid issue. The question remains though—how quickly and how well.

TEN

Baseball Management Contributed to the Abuse of Performance-Enhancing Drugs

Ryder Stevens

According to Ryder Stevens, Major League Baseball looked the other way when its star athletes were using performance-enhancing drugs in order to boost profits. He contends that when basic guidelines concerning drug use were established, no compulsory tests or punishments for infractions were included. Furthermore, he maintains, team physicians and trainers gave performance-enhancing drugs to ballplayers, who then started hitting the balls out of the ballpark. Stevens states that baseball had been in a slump with fans, but home run contests among the game's superstars drew the fans back in again. Stevens is a retired army chaplain who has taught leadership and ethics courses.

Between December's *Mitchell Report* and this month's [February 2008] congressional grilling of Roger Clemens, many of baseball's biggest names may have lost their ticket to the Hall of Fame. But all of the emphasis on players' use of performance-enhancing drugs misses a much bigger issue: Major League Baseball (MLB) itself took the performance-enhancing step of looking the other way in order to juice profits.

Ryder Stevens, "Why Baseball Balked at Integrity," *Christian Science Monitor*, February 25, 2008, p. 9. Copyright © 2008 The Christian Science Monitor. Reproduced by permission of the author.

To be sure, the players must be held accountable. Yet the more critical effort lies in restoring integrity to the baseball organization. To do that, Congress should stop refereeing he-said, he-said battles—and start working to replace baseball's commissioner with someone who can make wholesale changes.

Coming Late to the Battle

Compared with most other major professional sports, MLB was very late in defining banned substances, methods of testing, and punitive measures that would enforce compliance.

Major League Baseball commissioner Bud Selig (left) and executive director of the Major League Baseball Players Association Donald Fehr testify during the Mitchell hearings. The author says the commissioner, the owners, and the Players Association failed to provide drug-use guidelines and adequate testing practices between 1994 and 2005.

Why such procrastination? The 1994 season is a big part of the answer. That year, a player's strike cut the season short—there was no World Series. It was hugely damaging to fan confidence, and more important, to revenues. The strike cost owners millions of dollars in lost income.

After such a dismal year, the owners and the commissioner (Bud Selig, a former owner) needed to get the game going to make money again. The players, meanwhile, wanted to play and earn huge salaries. So they all tacitly agreed to postpone the moral necessity to set definitive standards for performance-enhancing drugs and the procedures for ensuring compliance or punishment.

MLB owners, their general managers, and players (the union) then created an environment from 1994 to 2005 where some guidelines were set but compulsory testing and punitive measures were lacking. Other professional and amateur sports already had these in place—some for more than a decade. MLB didn't implement random testing and severe consequences until 2006.

Employer-Provided Drugs

Consequently, any activity that happened before 2006 along the lines of steroids, human growth hormone (HGH), or other substances deemed to be "illegal" today is irrelevant. It's sad to consider how many professional athletes fell victim to these performance-enhancing temptations, but it's worth considering the larger context. Their employers provided them with all kinds of drugs (legally administered by team physicians and trainers) to speed their recovery after injuries. In the absence of strict measures, it's easy to see how many players took the next step of using drugs that were banned in other sports, yet not by MLB.

The years rolled by without any real efforts to get a policy in place. Why? Baseballs were leaving the ballpark in record numbers. Home run title quests were bringing folks back to the game. New fans filled the seats. Stars got huge contracts. Owners got lucrative cable television deals. MLB's business thrived; its leadership and ethics languished.

Baseball Attendance by Year

Reports of baseball players using steroids did not hurt attendance levels at ball games. Attendance rose each time star players were reported to be using steroids—particularly during 1998, when Mark McGwire and Sammy Sosa were in a race to see who would first surpass Major League Baseball's home run record of 61 home runs. Attendance levels went even higher in 2000 and remained high in 2001 when Barry Bonds, who had been dodging charges for years that he was using steroids, broke the home run record with 73 home runs. Attendance reached an all-time high in 2007 when Bonds broke the all-time home run record set by Hank Aaron in 1973.

1997	1998	1999	2000
62,899,062	70,601,147	70,103,204	72,702,420

2001	2002	2003	2004
72,567,108	67,944,389	67,630,052	72,968,953

2005	2006	2007	2008
74,385,295	75,959,167	79,447,312	78,584,286

Taken from: MLB Attendance, 2009. www.ballparksofbaseball.com..

Congress is partially culpable [guilty], too. MLB operates under a renewable exemption to the Sherman Antitrust Act that Congress grants. How can Congress continue to grant this exemption when baseball has failed the public trust so spectacularly?

The public hasn't been this outraged about America's pastime since the Black Sox scandal of 1919, when several Chicago White Sox players conspired with gamblers to "throw" the series. The backlash was severe—and the official response should guide policy today.

In 1920, the owners, realizing they had a huge problem, appointed the first commissioner of baseball: Judge Kenesaw

Landis, a federal judge from Chicago. This month [February 2008], in contrast, the owners gave commissioner Bud Selig an extension.

Time to Take Action

It is time for Congress to find a Judge Landis. Instead of holding hearings, Congress should take the reins of baseball away from the owners and replace the commissioner with a retired military officer of the highest rank. Generals Peter Pace or Eric Shinseki would fit the bill nicely. Both men are experienced in overhauling institutions and making them better. The commissioner's terms should be reviewed by the same congressional committee that renews the antitrust exemption.

Another possibility is to appoint an ombudsman [a person appointed to investigate, report on, and help settle complaints] who would be empowered to confidentially scrutinize baseball's enforcement of its drug policy. Names would not be the issue— just progress on the integrity of the sport that is part of the American fabric.

Without a house-cleaning, children across America will see another headline about a fallen baseball star and mutter, "Say it ain't so, Joe."

ELEVEN

Governments Must Become Involved in Fighting Performance-Enhancing Drugs

John Fahey

> John Fahey is the president of the World Anti-Doping Agency (WADA). According to Fahey in the following viewpoint, governments have the power, influence, and tools needed to fight performance-enhancing drugs in sport. He believes governments and law enforcement should share information about athletes who use drugs and force them to be removed from their sport. Fahey maintains that governments can establish and fund antidoping organizations and can promote programs educating youth and athletes about the dangers of performance-enhancing drugs.

Doping is a threat to public health and needs to be combated as such. Studies and surveys show alarming numbers. Once there is the perception that some elite athletes are using drugs in order to succeed in their sport, then the message is that, if you want to play at that level, you will have to do the same. That message trickles down and out, from the elite-level to college and junior athletes and still younger. And all of a sudden, you are not dealing with a few hundred, but instead a massive pyramid which has at its base hundreds of thousands of young people who believe that not only is it OK to dope, but that it is necessary in order to succeed.

The Importance of Governments

Last year [2008] I spoke about the importance of governments' role in the fight against doping. As a seasoned representative of governments with long experience in driving initiatives at the governmental level, I know the good that can come of greater engagement from governments worldwide in the harmonized fight against doping. Governments have the power, influence and tools to tackle some of the major issues that are outside of the purview of the Sport Movement.

I continue to say that, without full governmental engagement, we cannot effectively address laws and regulations at the national level that prohibit the actual manufacture, distribution and possession of these harmful substances. Without governments committed to cross-border cooperation in the name of anti-doping, we cannot effectively curtail the multiplication of networks of underground Internet marketing and trafficking of doping substances. In the same manner, the active engagement of government and law enforcement in sharing information and evidence with sport help ensure that those who might escape detection through testing will have their non-analytical anti-doping rule violations pursued so that they can be removed from sport.

Last year, I also told you about my belief that the solid foundations of the harmonized anti-doping system under the World Anti-Doping Code needed to be further strengthened by the Sport Movement, including through intensified education, research and targeted testing. I stressed that continued innovation needed to be implemented through new types of cooperation, new strategies and ideas borrowed from other fields.

So where has the fight against doping progressed in 2008?

2008 reflected the positive impact of the harmonization fostered by the World Anti-Doping Code, and showed a clear sign of the evolution of the fight against doping in sport promoted by WADA [the World Anti-Doping Agency]. I am confident that this evolution is helping us and will continue to help us protect the integrity of sport and the health of the athletes with ever more efficiency.

Governments Are More Involved

As a result of the Code implementation starting in 2004, more sports have started doing out-of-competition testing, as required by the Code. Governments have become more and more involved on many different levels, including supporting robust national testing programs. In fact, many of the numerous doping cases uncovered prior to the [2008] Beijing Olympic Games were the result of nations stepping up their testing efforts to ensure that the athletes they would send to Beijing were clean. Testing tactics themselves have gotten smarter with experience.

Under WADA's leadership, the traditional anti-doping model has also evolved from a strategy focusing only on the athlete and relying mainly on testing, research and education, to a new kind of model incorporating the athlete's entourage and the upstream elements of doping. I refer in particular to:

- combating production and trafficking of illegal substances;
- early detection of potentially performance-enhancing substances in development in cooperation with pharmaceutical companies; and
- evidence and information gathering and sharing between law enforcement and the Sport movement.

To me, this demonstrates that more and more governments and other key players not actively involved in this fight in the past have received the message that doping is wrong and is a major threat to greater public health.

Let me give you a few concrete examples of this evolution. As I am speaking today [February 24, 2009], 108 governments out of the 193 members of UNESCO [United Nations Educational, Scientific, and Cultural Organization] have ratified the International Convention against Doping in Sport, the legal tool they prepared and adopted to harmonize their laws and regulations with the World Anti-Doping Code. By UNESCO standards, this is by far the most successful ratification of any Convention within such a short time frame.

But the governmental contribution is far more than the simple ratification of a United Nations endorsed Convention. Throughout the world, governments are legislating, establishing and funding anti-doping organizations. They are also combating rogue manufacturing, marketing and trafficking of illegal substances. I am encouraged by the growing number of busts that are publicly reported. Only in the past few weeks, significant law enforcement operations and seizures were conducted in Slovenia, in Norway, in Australia, in Canada, in the United States, in Qatar, to take only a few examples. Underground laboratories and Web sites illegally marketing and selling controlled substances were shut down in several of these countries.

Working with Interpol

This willingness to limit the availability of illegal substances is part of the rationale behind the Memorandum of Understanding we formally signed earlier this month with Interpol, the world's largest police organization. This Memorandum of Understanding provides a framework for cooperation between our two organizations in tackling doping, in particular in evidence gathering and information sharing. The French government offered to seconde [provide] an officer to be based at Interpol's Headquarters in Lyon, France, to serve as the liaison between WADA, governments and the Sport movement, and the various Interpol bureaus around the world. WADA is very grateful to the French government for this contribution and to Interpol for partnering with us. We hope that this formalized cooperation will help achieve concrete advances.

Sharing Information

We are also finalizing protocols to facilitate evidence gathering and information sharing between governments and the Sport movement.

These various initiatives and actions are aimed at ensuring that the anti-doping community take full advantage of the possibility, set forth in the World Anti-Doping Code, to sanction "non-analytical" anti-doping rule violations, in other words violations that do involve a positive doping control but instead other evidence that an anti-doping rule violation occurred.

This is because many of the high profile doping cases and investigations in recent years have shown that government action and the sharing of information between law enforcement agencies and anti-doping organizations can be crucial in exposing anti-doping rule violations that would not have been detected

Joseph Blatter (right), president of the international governing association of the sport of football (soccer), and viewpoint author John Fahey, president of the World Anti-Doping Agency, shake hands after signing a letter of intent to strengthen international cooperation in the fight against doping.

through testing. Law enforcement and government agencies possess investigative powers to attack source and supply of illegal substances which sport does not have. In fact, the real strength of WADA lies precisely in the fact that it is a unique partnership between sport and public authorities, two groups that have a different and complementary set of powers and tools. . . .

Winning the Fight

So, are we winning the fight against doping in sport?

Yes, I believe we are on the right path. I believe that by federating the strengths of its stakeholders and by leading the global harmonized fight against doping, WADA has made a huge difference in its almost ten years of existence. This year, we are celebrating a decade of Play True. I believe that, with the commitment of and in collaboration with all those involved in this fight, we can continue to keep the momentum going forward.

There are, of course, challenges. Anti-doping science needs to keep up with the ever growing number of substances and techniques that may be misused and abused by cheaters, and with the rogue scientists and underground laboratories that may be trying to circumvent the system.

Major break-ups of massive manufacturing and trafficking rings confirm what we already knew, that doping is a crisis of international impact. But not all countries have the regulatory framework that allows law enforcement authorities to stem the rise of these nefarious schemes. All governments need to ensure they have laws in place that allow combating manufacturing, supply and possession of doping substances on their territories.

All countries need to be actively engaged in anti-doping. All countries need to accelerate the process of ratifying the UNESCO International Convention against Doping in Sport and apply its tenets. The absence of even one country from the fight against doping risks upsetting the balance sought for a level playing field. . . .

Education

Education efforts will need to be further stepped up. I am pleased that revisions to the Code have now made it mandatory for anti-doping organizations to implement education programs. I also believe the message is clear and understood by more athletes across all levels than ever before. But efforts need to be intensified.

Those who decide not to dope often do so because of personal convictions based on strong values such as respect, health, honour, dedication and hard work.

For us all to win the fight against doping, our children need to hear and adopt these universal values, as well as be given the tools to respond in the healthiest way when confronted with the question of doping. Our focus on early, values-based education, will help us to create a strong and stable anti-doping culture in which doping is prevented altogether.

Clean sport promotes responsible behaviour, observance of rules, discipline, respect of self and others, strength of character, tolerance and team spirit—all key values to be prized in a contributing member of society.

And sport is a microcosm of society—values that become entrenched and accepted by society at large will permeate sport and, at the same time, both the positive and negative aspects of sport will come to impact on society. Safeguarding clean sport is one way of working towards safeguarding the moral fabric and wellbeing of society at large.

All of us would be forgiven for believing the proliferation of doping over the years suggests that, for some, the currency placed on winning overrides the value of sport to teach the universal principles of respect, health, honour and dedication.

The Blemish of Deceit

For certain, every sport in every country have their share of fallen heroes whose medals now bear the blemish of deceit through doping. Only recently [American track and field athlete] Marion Jones was released from a US Prison, a sentence imposed on her for cheating in sport and then lying about it.

But what is the price that we in future generations pay if we were to ignore the cheats?

Lessons for Our Youth

Such attitudes towards sport unfortunately translate into lessons for our youth. Through these messages we are teaching our youngsters what is acceptable behaviour in modern society and in sport. Are we teaching youth that cheating is a violation of others rights? Or is the lesson rather that it matters only if you get caught?

It comes down to a simple, age-old truism: it is not whether you win or lose, but how you play the game. In life. In sport. In the junior leagues and the Olympics alike.

That is why it is so important to fight against the scourge of doping and send the message that doping is cheating, and cheat-

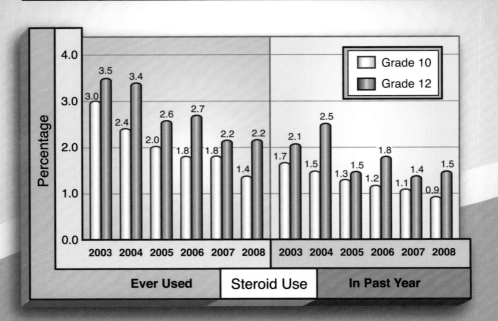

Fewer High School Students Are Using Steroids

Taken from: 2008 Monitoring the Future Survey. www.monitoringthefuture.org/data/08data/pr08t7.pdf.

ing is simply wrong. It violates the rights of clean athletes and it destroys the dignity and the health of those who dope.

We combat doping because we believe in the universal principles of truth, fairness, health, hard work and respect. And we believe it is our responsibility to preserve these values for our youth and the generations to come.

It may take a while to reach the finishing line in this fight, but I have no doubt we are much closer to that finishing line than we were last year and we will be even closer next year.

What You Should Know About Performance-Enhancing Drugs

What Performance-Enhancing Drugs Are

- Performance-enhancing drugs are hormones, including human growth hormone, steroids, amphetamines, and stimulants, or other substances used by athletes to improve their performance.
- Performance-enhancing drugs help an athlete build muscle faster and reduce the time needed to recover from strenuous workouts or from an injury.
- The most common steroids are anabolic (muscle-building) and androgenic (masculinizing). Different types of steroids are often taken together, in a technique known as stacking, in order to increase their effectiveness.
- Steroids and other performance enhancers are usually taken for a short period of time before the athlete reduces the dosage and then stops taking them for a few weeks. These cycles of on-again, off-again steroid use reduce the risk of negative side effects.
- Blood doping is considered a performance-enhancer and is also illegal. Blood doping means artificially increasing the number of red blood cells in an athlete's body by means of a transfusion or injection of real or synthetic blood. The extra red blood cells increase the amount of oxygen that is delivered to the muscles and thereby increases an athlete's endurance.

- Common slang names for performance-enhancing drugs are gear, Arnolds, gym candy, junk, 'roids, juice, and bulls.

Facts About Performance-Enhancing Drugs

- Some possible side effects of steroid abuse in men include infertility, breast development, shrinking of the testicles, and male-pattern baldness.
- Some possible side effects of steroid abuse in women include excessive growth of body hair, enlargement of the clitoris, and male-pattern baldness.
- A 2008 study of 375 international athletes found that nearly 10 percent had inadvertently taken a performance-enhancing drug, while 2.2 percent had knowingly taken a banned substance.
- Since 2000 steroid use in eighth- and tenth-graders has fallen steadily and has fallen among twelfth-graders since 2004. The 2008 *Monitoring the Future* survey found that only 0.9 percent of eighth- and tenth-graders had used steroids in the past year, and only 1.5 percent of twelfth-graders had.
- Steroid use steadily increases among men aged twenty-four and older. Nearly twice as many men aged twenty-nine to thirty (2.9 percent) have used steroids in the past year compared with men aged twenty-five to twenty-six (1.7 percent).
- An anonymous survey of professional baseball players found that between 5 percent and 7 percent of baseball players were taking performance-enhancing drugs in 2003.
- Of the 8,532 drug tests the U.S. Anti-Doping Agency performed in sixty-nine Olympic, Paralympic, and Pam American sporting competitions in 2008, twenty-five were positive. A first-time positive drug test results in a two-year suspension, followed by a lifetime ban for a subsequent positive test.
- A 2007 survey of American baseball fans found that 60 percent felt that Major League Baseball players who were named in the Mitchell Report as having used steroids and other performance-enhancing drugs should be punished; 43 percent said the punishment should include suspensions.

- In 2007 Major League Baseball instituted a drug policy that requires players who test positive for performance-enhancing drugs to be suspended for fifty games for a first offense, nearly one-third of a season's one hundred and sixty-two games.
- The National Football League began testing its players for steroids in 1987; the first year, 30 percent of its players tested positive for performance-enhancing drugs. Every football player is tested at least once a year for banned substances.
- National Basketball Association players who test positive for the first time are suspended for ten games; second offense, twenty-five games; third time, a year; fourth, banned for life.
- The National Hockey League allows its players to be randomly tested up to twice a year, with suspensions of twenty games, sixty games, and for life for drug use.
- The National Collegiate Athletic Association (NCAA) and the National Center for Drug Free Sport test all divisions of college athletes at individual and team championships. A positive test result earns a one-year suspension; a second positive test results in a loss of NCAA eligibility.

What You Should Do About Performance-Enhancing Drugs

The issues surrounding performance-enhancing drugs are complicated. Athletes take the drugs because they work; steroids and other performance-enhancing substances help athletes develop bigger and stronger muscles, give them more endurance, and help them recover from workouts and injuries faster. However, steroids and performance-enhancing drugs do have serious side effects, and in teens and young adults, these side effects can be irreversible. Most coaches, trainers, and doctors agree that it is dangerous and inappropriate for teens and young adults to take steroids and other performance enhancers. Opinions are sharply divided about whether adult athletes should take the drugs.

Examine Your Own Views

What motivates you? Under what circumstances might you use steroids? Would an honor code motivate you to stay clean? Would the threat of being suspended from your sport make you think twice about using steroids? Do schools have the right to test student athletes for steroid use? Do the policies at your school seem to be working? Are other students in your school using steroids? Are coaches and trainers and students looking the other way? Is that OK with you?

Understand the Rules

Adding to the confusion over the issue of performance-enhancing drugs is the fact that not all sports prohibit the same substances. What may be legal in one sport may be banned in another. Many collegiate and elite-level sports follow the guidelines of the World Anti-Doping Agency, which regulates which drugs and substances are banned in Olympic competitions. When androstenedione was discovered in Mark McGwire's locker in 1998, its use was permitted by Major League Baseball, although the National Football League, the National Collegiate Athletic Association, and the International Olympic Committee all banned it. Many athletes are confused about which drugs and substances are legal for them to take and which are not. Those athletes who are trying to stay honest will often call their league's hotline before they will take a prescribed or over-the-counter drug, just to make sure it is legal. The consequences for taking a banned substance are quite severe for Olympic and elite-level athletes; no leeway is given to athletes who claim they did not know the substance was illegal, or that they unknowingly took a banned drug, or that a legal substance was contaminated with an illegal substance. Athletes who do need a banned substance for a legitimate medical reason can apply for a Therapeutic Use Exemption. Athletes who are serious about staying clean make sure they are informed about everything they ingest or take into their bodies.

Make Healthy Decisions

Diet and exercise are the best and most important ways a teen athlete can get and stay in shape for sports. Everyone should eat a variety of healthy foods, and athletes especially should eat a variety of proteins, carbohydrates, calcium, vitamins and minerals, and fat. Lean red meats are a good source of amino acids, which the body breaks down to provide its own source of protein. Green leafy vegetables such as spinach, kale, mustard greens, and broccoli provide iron, calcium, and other much-needed vitamins and nutrients. Healthy bones need calcium, which is also found in dairy products such as milk and yogurt. Carbohydrates are another good source of fuel for the body. The fats found in cold-water fish, nuts, and olive, canola, and flaxseed oils, provide many health benefits.

Take a Stand

The articles in this volume will help you become more aware of the issues involved in using steroids and other performance-enhancing drugs. Get to know your school's policies on the use of performance-enhancing drugs. Coaches, trainers, and administrators want to know if their student athletes are taking steroids. As you become more informed, you can take a stand on steroid use in your school and in your sport. If you find that school authorities are turning a blind eye to steroid use, or if your school's policies do not seem fair or reasonable, do not be afraid to speak up. You may have insights that others may not have thought about. If you speak up in a respectful and reasoned way, administrators, coaches, and parents are more likely to consider your thoughts and opinions.

ORGANIZATIONS TO CONTACT

The editors have compiled the following list of organizations concerned with the issues debated in this book. The descriptions are derived from materials provided by the organizations. All have publications or information available for interested readers. The list was compiled on the date of publication of the present volume; the information provided here may change. Be aware that many organizations take several weeks or longer to respond to inquiries, so allow as much time as possible.

Association Against Steroid Abuse (AASA)
521 N. Sam Houston Pkwy. E., Ste. 635
Houston, TX 77060
Web site: www.steroidabuse.com

AASA is an educational organization that provides information and statistics on the dangers of anabolic steroid abuse. Its Web site includes information about steroid abuse, steroids and sports, the law, steroid myths, steroids and women, and different steroids.

National Center for Drug Free Sport
2537 Madison Ave.
Kansas City, MO 64108
(816) 474-8655
e-mail: info@drugfreesport
Web site: www.drugfreesport.com

The National Center for Drug Free Sport manages most aspects of the National Collegiate Athletic Association's drug-testing program. It also provides a Dietary Supplement Resource Exchange Center and a speaker's bureau. Its Web site includes recent news articles about drugs in sport and provides access to its quarterly magazine *Insight*.

National Clearinghouse for Alcohol and Drug Information
PO Box 2345
Rockville, MD 20847-2345
(800) 729-6686 or (301) 468-2600
e-mail: shs@health.org
Web site: www.health.org

The clearinghouse distributes publications of the U.S. Department of Health and Human Services, the National Institute on Drug Abuse, and other federal agencies concerned with alcohol and drug abuse. It provides reports, fact sheets, posters, and videos on steroid abuse, prevention, and treatment. Some of the publications are available on its Web site; others may be ordered at low cost.

National Collegiate Athletic Association (NCAA)
700 W. Washington St.
Indianapolis, IN 46206-6222
(317) 917-6222
Web site: www.ncaa.org

The NCAA oversees intercollegiate athletic programs and provides drug education and drug testing programs in partnership with the National Center for Drug Free Sport. Articles on performance-enhancing drugs are frequently published in the NCAA's twice-monthly online newsletter *NCAA News*.

National Institute on Drug Abuse (NIDA)
6001 Executive Blvd.
Bethesda, MD 20892-9561
(888) 644-6432 or (301) 443-1124
e-mail: information@nida.nih.gov
Web site: www.steroidabuse.org

NIDA supports and conducts research on drug abuse—including the yearly *Monitoring the Future Survey*—to improve drug abuse prevention, treatment, and policy efforts. It has a Web site devoted solely to anabolic steroid abuse, where it offers research reports and information about steroids. Information about steroids can also be found in its bimonthly *NIDA Notes* newsletter, the periodic "NIDA Capsules" fact sheets, and a catalog of research reports and public education materials, which can be found on NIDA's home page at www.drugabuse.gov.

National Strength and Conditioning Association (NSCA)
1885 Bob Johnson Dr.
Colorado Springs, CO 80906
(719) 632-6722
e-mail: nsca@nsca-lift.org
Web site: www.nsca-lift.org

The NSCA brings together strength and sport coaches, sport scientists, researchers, educators, physical therapists, physicians, athletic trainers, and personal trainers. The association provides educational resources and opportunities for its members and strives to develop and promote the profession of strength training and conditioning. Its Web site includes the position paper *Anabolic-Androgenic Steroid Use by Athletes and Code of Ethics* and an information packet for schools on combating anabolic steroid abuse.

Office of National Drug Control Policy
Executive Office of the President
Drugs and Crime Clearinghouse, PO Box 6000
Rockville, MD 20849-6000
e-mail: ondcp@ncjrs.org
Web site: www.whitehousedrugpolicy.gov

The Office of National Drug Control Policy is responsible for formulating the government's national drug strategy and the president's antidrug policy, as well as coordinating the federal agencies responsible for stopping drug trafficking. Information about steroids can be found on its Web site.

OHSU Health Promotion & Sports Medicine
3181 SW Sam Jackson Park Rd.
Portland, OR 97239-3098

(503) 418-4166
e-mail: chpr@ohsu.edu
Web site: www.ohsu.edu/hpsm/center.cfm

The Oregon Health and Science University Health Promotion and Sports Medicine offers two educational programs for coaches and trainers in schools, who then lead the programs for their athletes. ATLAS, geared for male athletes, and ATHENA, for female athletes, provide substance abuse prevention and information about healthy sports nutrition and strength training alternatives to illicit performance-enhancing drugs and alcohol.

Taylor Hooton Foundation
PO Box 2104
Frisco, TX 75034-9998
(972) 403-7300
e-mail: don.hooton@taylorhooton.org
Web site: www.taylorhooton.org

Founded in memory of Taylor Hooton, a high school athlete who committed suicide shortly after coming off a cycle of steroids, the foundation provides information about the dangers of anabolic steroid abuse and emphasizes prevention. The Web site offers educational resources and shares the tragic experiences of users and their families.

United States Anti-Doping Agency (USADA)
2550 Tenderfoot Hill St., Ste. 200
Colorado Springs, CO 80906-7346
(866) 601-2632 or (719) 785-2000
Web site: www.usantidoping.org

USADA is the national antidoping organization for the U.S. Olympics, Paralympics, and Pan American Games. USADA is responsible for testing athletes involved in these games for banned substances. Its antidoping program researches banned substances. USADA also offers an educational program to inform athletes, coaches, and trainers about policies, procedures, athletes' rights and responsibilities, and the dangers and consequences of using banned substances in sport.

United States Olympic Committee (USOC)
One Olympic Plaza
Colorado Springs, CO 80909
(719) 632-5551
e-mail: media@usoc.org
Web site: www.usoc.org

The USOC coordinates all Olympic-related activity in the United States. It works with the International Olympic Committee and other organizations to discourage the use of steroids and other drugs in sports. Information on USOC programs can be found on its Web site.

World Anti-Doping Agency (WADA)
800 Place Victoria, Ste. 1700, PO Box 120
Montreal, QC H4Z 1B7, Canada
(514) 904-9232
e-mail: info@wada-ama.org
Web site: www.wada-ama.org

WADA is an international independent organization created to promote, coordinate, and monitor the fight against doping in sport. It developed the World Anti-Doping Code, which sets antidoping policies, procedures, and regulations for all its participating nations. The code also includes the list of prohibited substances, exemptions for therapeutic use, rules for testing athletes, and procedures for protecting the athletes' privacy.

BIBLIOGRAPHY

Books

Shaun Assael, *Steroid Nation: Juiced Home Run Totals, Anti-Aging Miracles, and a Hercules in Every High School: The Secret History of America's True Drug Addiction.* New York: ESPN, 2007.

Howard Bryant, *Juicing the Game: Drugs, Power, and the Fight for the Soul of Major League Baseball.* New York: Viking, 2005.

Jose Canseco, *Juiced: Wild Times, Rampant 'Roids, Smash Hits, and How Baseball Got Big.* New York: HarperCollins, 2005.

Will Carroll, *The Juice: The Real Story of Baseball's Drug Problems.* Chicago: Ivan R. Dee, 2005.

Dan Clark, *Gladiator: A True Story of 'Roids, Rage, and Redemption.* New York: Scribner, 2009.

Mike Fainaru-Wada and Lance Williams, *Game of Shadows: Barry Bonds, BALCO, and the Steroids Scandal That Rocked Professional Sports.* New York: Gotham, 2006.

Nathan Jendrick, *Dunks, Doubles, Doping: How Steroids Are Killing American Athletics.* Guilford, CT: Lyons, 2006.

Jason W. Lee and Jeffrey C. Lee, eds., *Sport and Criminal Behavior.* Durham, NC: Carolina Academic Press, 2009.

John McCloskey and Julian Bailes, *When Winning Costs Too Much; Steroids, Supplements, and Scandal in Today's Sports.* Lanham, MD: Taylor Trade, 2005.

Dick Pound, *Inside Dope: How Drugs Are the Biggest Threat to Sports, Why You Should Care, and What Can Be Done About Them.* Mississauga, ON: John Wiley & Sons, 2006.

Teri Thompson et al., *American Icon: The Fall of Roger Clemens and the Rise of Steroids in America's Pastime.* New York: Knopf, 2009.

Periodicals

Nancy Armour, "Steroid's Problems Are Years Away," Associated Press, March 3, 2007.

Marky Billson, "Cheating in Baseball Is Old News," *Baseball Digest*, May 2008.

Randy Cohen, "Is Manny Ramirez Really All That Bad?" *New York Times*, May 19, 2009.

Danny Duncan Collum, "'I Yam What I Yam . . .' Except for Those Performance-Enhancing Drugs," *Sojourners*, June 15, 2007.

Brian Duffy, "Why Cutting Corners Comes as No Surprise," *U.S. News & World Report*, August 7, 2006.

David Epstein, "The Rules, the Law, the Reality," *Sports Illustrated*, February 16, 2009.

Michael Hiltzik, "Athletes, Steroids, and Public Hysteria," *Los Angeles Times*, March 2, 2009.

Patrick Hruby, "Let the Juicing Begin," *ESPN P.2*, March 10, 2006.

Bengt Kayser, Alexandre Mauron, and Andy Miah, "Viewpoint: Legalisation of Performance-Enhancing Drugs," *Lancet*, December 17, 2005.

Gwen Knapp, "Extreme Measures: Athletes Willing to Do Anything to Excel Are at Root of Problem," *San Francisco Chronicle*, July 23, 2006.

Michael LePage, "Only Drugs Can Stop the Sports Cheats," *New Scientist*, August 19, 2006.

Joe Lindsey, "Is There Another Way to Eliminate Doping?" *New York Times Freakonomics Blog*, January 29, 2008.

Mark McClusky, "Nix the Ban on Sports Drugs," *Wired*, September 21, 2005.

Edwin Moses, "Why Baseball Is in Denial," *Newsweek*, March 2, 2009.

Alva Noe, "A-Rod Isn't a Cheater," *Salon*, May 1, 2009.

Alice Park, "What's Driving Dara Torres," *Time*, August 4, 2008.

Joe Posnanski, "Home Run Numbers Have Totally Lost Their Mystique," *Sports Illustrated*, June 17, 2009.

Ken Rosenthal, "Coming Clean," *Sporting News*, June 10, 2005.

Marissa Saltzman, "Chemical Edge: The Risks of Performance-Enhancing Drugs," *Odyssey*, May 2006.

Kate Schmidt, "Steroids: Take One for the Team," *Los Angeles Times*, October 14, 2007.

Abraham Socher, "No Game for Old Men," *Commentary*, March 2008.

Phil Taylor, "Baseball Needs a New Boss," *Sports Illustrated*, May 18, 2009.

Tom Verducci, "The Night the Lights Went Out in Mannywood," *Sports Illustrated*, May 18, 2009.

INDEX

McNamee, Brian, 18, 21
McNeil, Sally, 13
Mencken, H.L., 33, 40
Merriman, Shawne, 8
Miller, Bode, 60
Mitchell, George, 18, *76*
Mitchell Report (2007), 18, 19–20, 22–23, 75–77, 79, 80
MLB. *See* Major League Baseball
Münzer, Andreas, 14

N
New York Times (newspaper), 22, 23

O
Olympic Games
  doping control lab of, *52*
  medals recalled from athletes due to doping during, *52*
Opinion polls. *See* Surveys

P
Pelletier, David, *29*, *30*
Performance-enhancing drugs
  amateur athletes and, *62*
  do not belong in sports, 59–66
  few athletes admit to use of, *47*
  governments must become involved in fighting use of, 85–93
  MLB management contributed to abuse of, 80–84

Olympic athletes and, *30*
prevalence of use, 7
should be allowed in sports, 49–58
use in sports is cheating, 25–32, 92–93
use in sports is not cheating, 33–40
See also Amphetamines; Human growth hormone; Steroids
Plaschke, Bill, 7
Polls. *See* Surveys
Pope, Harrison, 13
Pound, Richard W., 25, 38, 39
Psychotropic drugs, 15

R
Ramirez, Manny, 5–7, *6*, 8
Riccardi, John, 12
Rodriguez, Alex, 8
Rogers, Shaun, 8
'Roid rage, 11–13
Romanowski, Bill, 8
Rose, Pete, 77
Rude, Ravishing Rick, 14
Ruth, Babe, 61

S
Salé, Jaime, *29*, *30*
Selig, Bud, 18, *81*, 84
Sheen, Fulton, 32
Sherman Antitrust Act (1890), MLB exemption to, 83

PICTURE CREDITS